Tracking Serial Killers

by Diane Yancey

LUCENT BOOKS

An imprint of Thomson Gale, a part of The Thomson Corporation

THOMSON
✳
GALE

Detroit • New York • San Francisco • New Haven, Conn. • Waterville, Maine • London

LIBRARY OF CONGRESS CATALOGING-IN-PUBLICATION DATA

Yancey, Diane.
  Tracking serial killers / by Diane Yancey.
    p. cm. — (Crime scene investigations)
  Includes bibliographical references and index.
  ISBN 978-1-59018-985-6 (hardcover)
  1. Serial murder investigation—United States—Juvenile literature. 2. Serial murderers—United States—Psychology—Juvenile literature. 3. Criminal behavior, Prediction of—United States—Juvenile literature. I. Title.
  HV8079.H6Y35 2007
  363.25'9523—dc22
                                                                      2007006813

ISBN-10: 1-59018-985-X
Printed in the United States of America

Contents

Foreword

The popularity of crime scene and investigative crime shows on television has come as a surprise to many who work in the field. The main surprise is the concept that crime scene analysts are the true crime solvers, when in truth, it takes dozens of people, doing many different jobs, to solve a crime. Often, the crime scene analyst's contribution is a small one. One Minnesota forensic scientist says that the public "has gotten the wrong idea. Because I work in a lab similar to the ones on *CSI*, people seem to think I'm solving crimes left and right—just me and my microscope. They don't believe me when I tell them that it's the investigators that are solving crimes, not me."

Crime scene analysts do have an important role to play, however. Science has rapidly added a whole new dimension to gathering and assessing evidence. Modern crime labs can match a hair of a murder suspect to one found on a murder victim, for example, or recover a latent fingerprint from a threatening letter, or use a powerful microscope to match tool marks made during the wiring of an explosive device to a tool in a suspect's possession.

Probably the most exciting of the forensic scientist's tools is DNA analysis. DNA can be found in just one drop of blood, a dribble of saliva on a toothbrush, or even the residue from a fingerprint. Some DNA analysis techniques enable scientists to tell with certainty, for example, whether a drop of blood on a suspect's shirt is that of a murder victim.

While these exciting techniques are now an essential part of many investigations, they cannot solve crimes alone. "DNA doesn't come with a name and address on it," says the Minnesota forensic scientist. "It's great if you have someone in custody to match the sample to, but otherwise, it doesn't help. That's the investigator's job. We can have all the great DNA evidence in the world, and without a suspect, it will just sit on the shelf. We've all seen cases with very little forensic evidence get solved by the resourcefulness of a detective."

While forensic specialists get the most media attention today, the work of detectives still forms the core of most criminal investigations. Their job, in many ways, has changed little over the years. Most cases are still solved through the persistence and determination of a criminal detective whose work may be anything but glamorous. Many cases require routine, even mind-numbing tasks. After the July 2005 bombings in London, for example, police officers sat in front of video players watching thousands of hours of closed-circuit television tape from security cameras throughout the city, and as a result were able to get the first images of the bombers.

The Lucent Books Crime Scene Investigations series explores the variety of ways crimes are solved. Titles cover particular crimes such as murder, specific cases such as the killing of three civil rights workers in Mississippi, or the role specialists such as medical examiners play in solving crimes. Each title in the series demonstrates the ways a crime may be solved, from the various applications of forensic science and technology to the reasoning of investigators. Sidebars examine both the limits and possibilities of the new technologies and present crime statistics, career information, and step-by-step explanations of scientific and legal processes.

The Crime Scene Investigations series strives to be both informative and realistic about how members of law enforcement—criminal investigators, forensic scientists, and others—solve crimes, for it is essential that student researchers understand that crime solving is rarely quick or easy. Many factors—from a detective's dogged pursuit of one tenuous lead to a suspect's careless mistakes to sheer luck to complex calculations computed in the lab—are all part of crime solving today.

With Lethal Intent

In 1978 citizens of Wichita, Kansas, lived in fear as a serial killer who called himself BTK—for Bind, Torture, and Kill—stalked their neighborhoods, broke into homes, and subjected his victims to slow and painful deaths. To protect themselves, homeowners bought security systems and guns. They boarded over backyard windows and doors of their homes and routinely checked for cut phone lines. Women refused to shut closet doors after learning that the attacker sometimes hid in closets, waiting to strike.

The police followed thousands of leads and checked out numerous suspects to no avail. In 2005, however, officials were able to catch the killer with the aid of DNA and advanced technology. He turned out to be a former Cub Scout leader named Dennis Rader, a family man who had lived in the Wichita area all his life. For those who had tracked him, the arrest justified all their years of frustration and hard work. "This is the first time we've been able to see a light at the end of this very, very, very long tunnel,"[1] said Wichita police lieutenant Kenneth Landwehr one day after the arrest.

Most Notorious

Although Dennis Rader gained widespread notoriety for his crimes, he was not the first killer to take the lives of multiple victims in the United States. In the early 1800s Samuel Green rampaged through New England, raping, stealing, and murdering until he was arrested and hanged in 1822. In 1893 Herman Webster Mudgett, also known as H.H. Holmes, trapped, tortured, and murdered women who stayed as guests at the Chicago hotel he had opened for the World's Columbian

H.H. Holmes was one of the earliest known serial killers, convicted of killing twenty-seven people in 1896.

Serial killer Aileen Wuornos is an exception to the general rule that serial killers are male.

What Makes a Serial Killer?

No one knows why some men and women become serial killers. Yet there are events that seem to be influential, as the editors of Mob Magazine *explain in an online article entitled "Serial Killers, Why They Kill?":*

A large percent of serial killers suffer abuse early in life. Some of their stories are horrific. Many have sustained head injuries early in their lives or have some minor form of congenital [inherited] deformity. Most describe themselves as outsiders. They were usually picked on by their peers and had more than the usual insecurities with the opposite sex. Around seventy-five percent of all serial killers describe being in sexually uncomfortable situations or environments when growing up. Yet, most people that suffer the same tragedies in their lives do not become killers.

All in all there is no firm medical explanation for why a serial killer becomes a serial killer. Maybe there is a certain experience cocktail that leads a person to extreme violence, but it has yet to be pin pointed.

Mob Magazine, "Serial Killers, Why They Kill?" www.mobmagazine.com/manage article.asp?c=120&a=7222.

Exposition. In 1896 he confessed to twenty-seven murders in Chicago, Indianapolis, and Toronto, Canada, but officials believe he may have murdered as many as one hundred.

Other notorious American serial killers followed Mudgett. Albert Fish ate the flesh of children he murdered between 1919 and 1935. Edmund Kemper killed and dismembered six female hitchhikers in California before murdering his mother in 1973. Aileen Wuornos took the lives of at least six men in 1989 and 1990 and was considered something of a rarity because most serial killers are male.

Male or female, serial killers are not limited to the United States. A Frenchwoman named Locusta poisoned ancient Romans during the first century A.D. Jack the Ripper murdered and mutilated at least five prostitutes in London in 1888. Ukrainian Andrei Chikatilo, nicknamed the Rostov Ripper, killed at least fifty-three women and children in Asia. His prolonged campaign of serial murder began in 1978 and continued until 1990.

"Sing the Die Song"

The fact that Chikatilo, Rader, and others were able to evade authorities for decades emphasizes the difficulty law enforcement officials have identifying and catching serial killers. They are much better at labeling and defining them. By definition, serial killers are men or women who have taken the lives of at least three victims over an extended period of time.

Their victims are usually vulnerable strangers, such as young people and prostitutes, whom they can control and on whom they act out their brutal fantasies. Prostitutes are particularly popular targets because there is little public outcry when they are killed.

Most serial killers murder for pleasure rather than profit. Why they love to kill is open to debate. Some experts believe upbringing is the key; they cite statistics that show that many killers come from dysfunctional families and are mentally and emotionally scarred in some way. Edmund Kemper, for instance, was shamed and humiliated by his domineering mother. Aileen Wuornos was physically and sexually abused as a child.

Edmund Kemper's dysfunctional relationship with his mother may have triggered the rage that compelled him to kill women in the Santa Cruz area in 1972 and 1973.

9

By the Numbers

$3 MILLION

Average cost of an execution in the United States.

Some experts believe killers are influenced by impersonal Western society with its emphasis on sex and violence. It is a desensitizing factor in the lives of those who have the inclination to kill. Still other experts insist that at least part of the problem stems from the killers' physical or mental makeup. Mental illness may run in their families, or they may have suffered a serious accident. Author Shirley Lynn Scott observes, "Herbert Mullin, Santa Cruz killer of thirteen, blamed the voices in his head that told him it was time to 'sing the die song,' . . . while Bobby Joe Long said a motorcycle accident made him hypersexual and eventually a serial lust killer."[2]

Whether serial killers are born or created, their numbers seem to be growing. From the 1920s to the 1950s, multiple murders were rare in the United States, although the low number might have been due to a low incidence of reporting. During the 1960s it was estimated that one new multiple killer was reported every twenty months, and the number jumped to one every seven months in the 1970s. From 1980 to 1984 a new multiple murderer was reported every 1.8 months. Crime figures from 1982 to 1989 indicated a 270 percent increase in serial murder in the United States, compared to a 12 percent increase in general murder over the same period.

Patience and Persistence

No matter what factors cause serial killers to kill, everyone agrees that they are difficult to catch. This is partly because they are experts at taking lives. They give it much thought, perfect their strategies, and learn from their mistakes. For instance, Wayne Williams, who is believed to have killed at least twenty-two children in Atlanta, Georgia, between 1979 and 1981, began dumping bodies in a nearby river after learning that authorities had found evidence on his previous victims.

Robert Lee Yates Jr., who took the lives of at least thirteen women in Spokane, Washington, between 1996 and 1998, increased the number of shopping bags he placed over his victims' heads in order to ensure that he did not become covered with their blood.

Serial killers also avoid capture because they usually appear totally normal to those around them. Rather than acting like

Crimes in a Series

There is debate over who invented the term serial killer, *but both Robert K. Ressler and Robert D. Keppel began using the expression in the 1970s. In his book* Whoever Fights Monsters, *coauthored with Tom Shachtman, Ressler explains how he came up with the phrase.*

[I was often asked to lecture overseas, and] it was at one of these international sessions that I coined the term serial killer, now much in use. At that time, killings such as those of 'Son of Sam' killer David Berkowitz in New York were invariably labeled 'stranger killings.' This term didn't seem appropriate to me, however, for sometimes killers do know their victims. Various other terms had also been used, but none hit the nail on the head. I'd been invited to participate in a week of lectures at Bramshill, the British police academy, and while there, I took the opportunity to attend the other seminars and lectures. In one of them, a man was discussing what the Brits called crimes in series— a series of rapes, burglaries, arsons, murders. That seemed a highly appropriate way of characterizing the killings of those who do one murder, then another and another in a fairly repetitive way, and so in my classes at [the FBI academy at] Quantico, [Virginia,] and elsewhere I began referring to 'serial killers.'

Robert K. Ressler and Tom Shachtman, *Whoever Fights Monsters: My Twenty Years Tracking Serial Killers for the FBI.* New York: St. Martin's, 1992, p. 32.

Wayne Williams became harder to catch when he began dumping the bodies of his young victims in the river after learning that the police had found evidence on his previous victims.

the wild-eyed maniacs that people expect killers to be, most are calm, friendly, and ordinary. Many hold jobs and have families and friends. As Gary Van Dusen says of his neighbor, Dennis Rader, "[His arrest was] the biggest shock I'd ever had—[he was] the nicest guy in the world. I'd have given him a key to watch my dog if I had to when I was leaving town."[3] If, by chance, such killers come to the notice of the police and are taken in for questioning, they are often cooperative and are able to pass polygraph tests, primarily because they feel no guilt for the crimes they have committed.

Tracking serial killers who have the advantage of time and anonymity is an enormous challenge for law enforcement officers. All accept the challenge, however, when a killer appears in their region. They believe they will eventually be able to catch the killer, particularly if they utilize a broad range of techniques that have been developed by earlier investigators. These techniques range from creating psychological profiles to accessing high-tech forensic databases (organized collections of information stored in computers).

While they hunt, investigators also know that persistence and good luck will be as important as any crime lab or computer database. Thus, as they focus on their task, they ask the public to be patient with their efforts. David Reichert, who tracked the Green River Killer in Washington State, observes, "Many people have an unrealistic view of police work. They believe that we can solve any crime if we only try hard enough. We do have good investigators and a few tools at our disposal. . . . But the miracle discoveries you see in the movies and on TV rarely happen in real life."[4]

CHAPTER 1

Monster Hunters

Everyone knows that serial killers can be found anywhere, but police officers sometimes find it hard to recognize that one is at large in their region. They may find one body, then another a few weeks or months later, and then another. The killer may confuse them by changing his method of operating. The first victim could be a middle-aged female, whereas the next two could be young. The first could be strangled, the next two stabbed. Bodies may be deposited in different police jurisdictions so that no one notices that the number of killings is growing.

Even after several similar homicides have occurred, police might deny that they are connected. They might refuse to check and see if there are related murders in other jurisdictions. This denial is termed *linkage blindness* and can stem from the fact that they are unwilling to face that they have a serial killer on their hands. They know tracking such a killer is likely to be a long and discouraging process. It will mean asking others for help. It will stir up unpleasant media attention and cause everyone to demand that the killer be caught quickly. Rather than deal with such pressure, they would rather downplay the problem, try to handle it quickly and quietly, and get it over with.

Downplaying the problem never catches the killer, however, and linkage blindness always plays directly into his or her hands. Psychologist Jan Bouchard-Kerr notes, "'Linkage blindness' has allowed serial killers to go on murdering months and sometimes years longer because it has delayed alerting the public to the danger of an active serial predator and the mobilization of police resources to catch the murderer."[5]

Detectives review the clue board during the hunt for Son of Sam in New York City. At one point, approximately three hundred officers were assigned to the case.

The Task Force

Once authorities determine that they are hunting a serial killer, they commonly form a task force that can concentrate on catching the perpetrator. Crime profiler John Philpin writes, "The purpose of a homicide task force is to facilitate the work of investigators. At best, the task force centralizes information and provides the clerical and computer support officers need. At worst, the task force becomes a venue [setting] for performing personalities."[6]

Depending on where a serial killer strikes, the size of the task force can be large or small. In New York City in the 1970s, for instance, some three hundred police officers were dedicated to catching the Son of Sam killer. In Seattle, Washington,

With only two years' experience in the major crimes unit, Dave Reichert became the lead detective on the Green River Killer case in Seattle.

the Green River Killer task force ranged from twenty-five to fifty members. In smaller towns, such as Spokane, Washington, or Salem, Oregon, a handful of men and women might be all that can be spared from other law enforcement duties.

The numbers are often increased when dead bodies are found in several jurisdictions. Then each department involved generally assigns several investigators to the case, and the task force becomes a multi-agency association. In the hunt for the so-called Hillside Strangler in the Los Angeles area in the late 1970s, the Los Angeles Police Department, the Glendale Police Department, and the Los Angeles County Sheriff's Department teamed up to catch what turned out to be two killers: Kenneth Bianchi and his cousin Angelo Buono Jr. The two men were eventually found guilty of killing more than seven women in California and Washington. In Louisiana between 2001 and 2003, the Baton Rouge Police Department, East Baton Rouge Parish Sheriff's Department, Lafayette Parish Sheriff's Department, and the Iberville Parish Sheriff's Department, as well as Louisiana State Police and the Federal Bureau of Investigation (FBI), worked together to track down Derrick Todd Lee, who allegedly killed five women throughout the state.

Ideally, a task force is made up of the most experienced homicide detectives and forensic experts available. In Wichita, Kansas, when the BTK strangler was at large, the first team formed to track him was nicknamed the Hot Dog Squad because of the confidence of its members and their reputations for handling tough cases. Detective Bernie Drowatsky, for instance, had been Wichita's Police Officer of the Year in 1973 after he caught another serial killer, Thomas Leo McCorgary.

Many times, however, no serial killer expert is available in the department. Then ordinary homicide detectives take up the challenge. In Washington State, for instance, the Green River Killer task force included lead detective David Reichert, who had been in the King County Police Department's major crimes unit less than two years, and Detective Sue Peters, who was twenty-four and a new hire of the department.

Paperwork

The purpose of the task force is to work full-time centralizing information and focusing on multiple aspects of the investigation. This includes keeping records, investigating missing-person reports, processing crime scenes, interviewing witnesses and suspects, following up on tips that are mailed or phoned in, and communicating with experts and other law enforcement personnel throughout the country.

Record keeping alone often becomes a full-time job because of the enormous amounts of evidence and information that is collected in the course of a case. Crime writer Ann Rule describes the Green River files seven years into the investigation: "Try to imagine your own life, as if you had pressed every corsage, saved every letter, taken photos of every piece of jewelry you ever owned, every garment, dirt samples from the yard of every residence, . . . all the artifacts of your days on earth. Each victim's section was at least two thousand pages long; some were ten times that count."[7]

Usually one or more members make record keeping their primary focus so that a confusion of items and paperwork does not slow the case. Lieutenant Stanley Bachman, who worked on the Hillside Strangler case, explains: "Every piece of information that came in regarding the [murders], or any inquiries regarding whatever, went to the same . . . two or three people who were assigned to answer the phones. And they kept a log on everything so that you could go back and trace it."[8]

Prior to the widespread use of personal computers, task forces stored records in file cabinets and relied on paper graphs and wall charts to correlate information. Computers made the filing and correlating easier. Once information is entered, data

Good Training and Good Luck

Serial killers are often extremely difficult to catch, and a task force must do an exceptional job if it is going to bring such killers to justice. Expert Robert D. Keppel explains in a 2005 Internet article entitled "Serial Murder" found on the Crime Library Web site:

With the [successful cases] that I've seen, it's a combination of good police work, on the part of uniformed police officers, and the ability to have an investigative force that recognizes when that traffic stop or a contact with that police officer turns into a lead that they can develop.... I always say that most of the time it's luck because some police officer has stopped [the killer] or come across them in some other uniform situation, but it also takes the investigators in the background, either in a task force or working on a case, to pick up and recognize the information that could lead to the resolution of the case. That's one thing with a lot of these cases—when they become known to law enforcement, it's usually through the uniformed officers. How they categorize their information and use it is a different story. It takes a decent investigative force to take that information and make it something valuable.

Robert D. Keppel, "Serial Murder," Crime Library. www.crimelibrary.com/criminal_mind/profiling/keppel1/7.html.

can be pulled up and viewed with the tap of a few keys. Investigators can see connections between suspects, victims, times, and locales that they might otherwise overlook. Once in a while, those connections lead to the killer. In 1987, when Task Force member Matthew Haney pulled up information on suspect Gary Ridgway, a truck painter who frequented prostitutes, he noticed that Ridgway had had prior contact with several of the victims. He was also able to determine that

Ridgway had been off work when all of the killings took place. Although that information was not enough to lead to an arrest at the time, it was used in 2001 to get Ridgway to confess to forty-eight murders.

Searching for Leads

In addition to centralizing and coordinating information, task force members must follow up on missing-person reports to get leads on the victims. This vital part of the investigation is often the most frustrating because the missing can be prostitutes, hitchhikers, runaway teens, and others who are often seen as transients or social outcasts. Their disappearance may not be reported promptly, or, if it is, police officers may not follow up because they assume the missing may have simply moved to another city or state. Thus, task force members often find that the exact time or place of the disappearance cannot be determined.

Without that information, they are unable to seek useful facts, such as what the killer looked like, the hours he hunted his victims, the kind of car he drove, and so forth. Former police detective Michael Nault, who was part of two serial murder investigations in Washington State, says, "There is no more important nexus [link] to find serial killers than missing persons. The major things done wrong in the Ted Bundy and Green River cases were failures to track and identify missing persons."[9]

Task force members attempt to determine the killer's general area of operation and focus on that locale. They try to find witnesses who might have seen victims talking to a suspicious stranger or being dragged into a car. In the case of the Green River Killer, who targeted street prostitutes between 1982 and 2001, detectives canvassed a seedy section of highway known as the Strip, where young women loitered when soliciting their customers. In the case of killer Jerry Brudos, who targeted college women in and around Salem, Oregon, in 1968 and 1969, detectives focused on dormitories on the nearby Oregon State University campus, interviewing dozens of college students to see if they had any information to contribute. Ann Rule observes, "Asking questions is a major part of a detective's work. A million answers may be utterly useless, and a thousand possible witnesses have to be dismissed. . . . But the right answer cannot be jarred free unless a concerted effort is made. When that one answer shines through, it is worth all the tedium."[10]

Tricky Business

Interviewing witnesses requires patience and psychology. Although investigators must remain professional, they also need to appear sympathetic and nonjudgmental. With women who are prostitutes and/or drug users, they have to work hard to convince them that they will not be arrested if they admit to illegal activity. Usually, at least a few women put their suspicions aside and supply valuable information. For instance, in the Yates case in Spokane, several prostitutes reported being

Police officers must be careful when interviewing possible witnesses to ensure they get correct and timely information about crimes.

13

Age at which America's youngest serial killer, Craig Price, committed his first murder.

approached by a sinister man who later proved to be the killer. Other women remain unconvinced, however, preferring to take their chances with the killer rather than trust authorities. Journalist Chet Rogers observes, "The cops are the law, and prostitutes are lawbreakers. It's hard for prostitutes to turn to the cops for protection when the cops' duties often include arresting them."[11]

Interviewing suspects and persons of interest is just as challenging as interviewing witnesses. If the wrong technique is used and a suspect becomes belligerent, investigators are not likely to ever learn anything useful. They may also cause additional complications. When task force members and FBI agents took construction worker Ernest W. "Bill" McLean into custody in 1985, searched his home, and pressured him to confess to the Green River killings, McLean became embarrassed and angry. The fact that he was almost immediately cleared did not stop the media from publishing his name and stating he was a suspect. McLean filed a lawsuit against area newspapers, claiming they had damaged his reputation, and the public reacted against the apparent incompetence of the task force. At the time, Seattleite Sherri Rogalski wrote in an editorial in the *Seattle Times*, "By involving the media prior to the filing of charges, the Task Force showed little regard for McLean's personal rights. Such vigilante tactics are an affront to us all."[12]

In an effort to avoid problems, investigators like to begin an interview by complimenting the suspect and asking for his help. They then determine if he is likely to respond to friendliness, flattery, or firmness and try to use the appropriate approach. Arlyn Smith, former member of the BTK task force, says, "You have to be pretty intuitive about people. When you find something that works, keep doing that."[13]

Processing Crime Scenes

Whereas some members of the task force exercise their "people skills" in interviews, others focus on processing crime scenes that are an integral part of any serial murder case. The work begins as soon as a body is found. As they approach it, detectives know they must be careful not to disturb any evidence, so they usually tread a narrow path from their vehicles, checking all the while to be sure that nothing important is lying underfoot. If there are indications that more than one body may be on site—the discovery of two skulls, for instance—crime-scene tape is quickly strung around a wide perimeter to block possible trespassers. Within the perimeter, tape is also strung around each decomposition site, or set of remains. Another circle of tape is strung around the areas where remains might have been scattered by weather or animals.

Following those steps, each decomposition site is carefully examined. Sometimes the process can take three or four days.

Investigators mark a crime scene with crime-scene tape to prevent contamination of any evidence they might find there.

Police officers thoroughly investigate crime scenes such as this one where the Hillside Strangler's thirteenth victim was found.

Photos and videos are taken throughout. A medical examiner, responsible for determining manner of death and identity of the victim, examines the remains. These are then collected for a later autopsy in the lab. All the while, investigators search the site on hands and knees, using magnifying glasses and tweezers to collect trace evidence such as hair, fingernails, and bits of bone. Vegetation over and around the body is cut down and checked for evidence. A metal detector is sometimes used to ensure that metallic objects such as jewelry are not overlooked.

While decomposition sites are being processed, other investigators search the entire crime scene for evidence the killer might have left behind. This is an extremely difficult task if the area is overgrown or if the killer deposits his victims where others have dumped trash and debris. Investigators must try to decide whether articles such as cigarette butts, rags, and beer cans are evidence. Author Ted Schwarz writes of one of the early crime scenes in the Hillside Strangler case, "No one knew what the case might eventually prove to be. Until they had more details concerning the death, . . . everything had to be assumed to be significant."[14]

Every article that seems significant is photographed and then carefully placed in a bag to prevent contamination. It is also given a number and logged in order to correctly preserve it for a later trial. Investigators then transport it to the crime lab for further analysis.

Outside Help

Because task force members may not know exactly what techniques to use when they begin their hunt for a killer, they regularly tap into the wisdom and skill of a host of experts, including the FBI and police officers who have worked other serial murder cases. In 1978, for instance, the first BTK task force talked to New York detectives who had investigated the Son of Sam case, as well as to members of the Los Angeles Police Department who were tracking the Hillside Strangler. Wichita police chief Richard LaMunyon recalls, "[We] talked to other agencies to solicit how

Tools of the Trade

Crime scene investigators could not perform their duties without a crime kit including the following vital tools:

1. **magnifying lens, scissors, tweezers, and scalpel**
2. **tape measure**
3. **rulers of different lengths**
4. **safety equipment (gloves, masks, boots, etc.)**
5. **camera**
6. **notepad**
7. **flashlight**
8. **an alternate light source**
9. **chemical reagents such as luminol that reveal blood**
10. **evidence seals, tags, bags, envelopes, and boxes of different sizes**

they have handled their investigations, basically, just to shed some light on methods."[15]

Former Seattle police officer Robert D. Keppel, an associate professor of criminal justice at Sam Houston State University in Huntsville, Texas, is a valued consultant on many cases. Keppel was one of the lead investigators in the Theodore "Ted" Bundy case in Washington State in the 1970s. Bundy eluded Keppel and moved on to Utah, where he was convicted of kidnapping in 1975. He twice escaped from prison and fled to Florida, where he murdered three more young women before being caught. Bundy eventually confessed to over thirty murders in Washington, Utah, Colorado, and Florida between 1974 and 1978; he was executed in 1989.

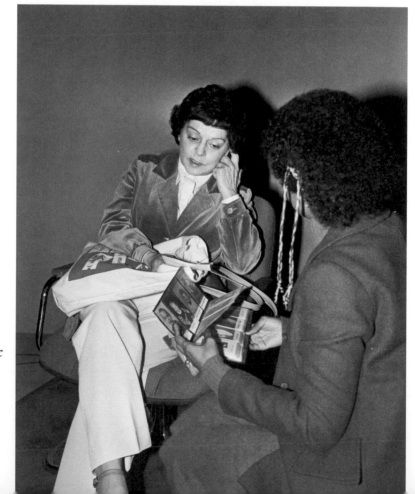

Atlanta police officers recruited high-profile psychic Dorothy Allison (left) to help them solve the Atlanta Child Murders.

Locard's Exchange Principle

Every member of a task force keeps Locard's exchange principle in mind when processing a crime scene. The principle was formulated by twentieth-century forensic scientist Edmond Locard, who was the director of the world's first crime laboratory in Lyon, France. He determined from observation that when there is contact between two items, there will be an exchange of some sort. For instance, when a man sits on a sofa, a fiber or two from his clothing is likely to remain behind. When he walks across a yard, dirt particles will adhere to the soles of his shoes and then will be left on the carpet of the next house he enters.

When applied to crime scenes, Locard's principle means that the perpetrator of a crime will probably leave a piece of evidence at the scene in addition to carrying something away. His saliva will be left on the victim's skin. A hair from the head of the victim will stick to his pant leg and be carried to the seat of his car. As Locard emphasized, every contact leaves a trace, and everyone on the task force—from investigators to crime lab analysts—knows that it is his or her job to find it.

While working the Bundy investigation, Keppel pioneered many methods used today to track serial killers. These include the use of Explorer Search and Rescue scouts to search for evidence at a crime scene and use of the most up-to-date computer systems as organizational tools and time-savers. After leaving the police force, Keppel went on to consult on hundreds of serial murder cases, including the Atlanta Child Murders and the Green River Killer investigation.

Experts like Keppel are welcomed by all law enforcement authorities for the insight they have and the suggestions they give, but other types of consultants are more controversial. These include psychics, numerologists, astrologers, and hypnotists who may be called in when a case stalls and all other options fail. Most task force members scorn whatever these controversial practitioners have to offer, but some authorities become desperate enough to try anything if it means catching the killer. Thus, the Boston Strangler task force called in Dutch psychic Peter Hurkos in 1963 in an effort to learn who was killing women in the Boston area. Atlanta, Georgia, officials consulted high-profile psychic Dorothy Allison in 1980 when trying to solve their serial killer case. The BTK task force sent eyewitnesses to a hypnotist in 1988 to try to get more details regarding a man they believed to be the killer. Despite lengthy sessions and a great deal of effort, none of the consultants was able to further the investigations.

The Green River task force allowed dowsers (individuals who seek water in the ground with a forked stick) to try to locate bodies in the course of its case. It also tolerated the presence of psychic Barbara Kubic-Patten, who closely followed them around and was credited with discovering one of the victims in 1984. Task force commander Frank Adamson, who was skeptical of Kubic-Patten's powers, recalls, "She had to go quite a ways into a copse [grove] of alder trees . . . to find the body. The remains were covered with a green plastic garbage bag. . . . It was rather remarkable that she *did* find it."[16]

Fighting Despair

While task force members become skilled at tracking killers whom they see as heartless "monsters," they do not become coldhearted themselves. Rather, memories of the victims haunt them. They feel compelled to spend every waking moment on the case to the neglect of their own health and mental well-being. Spokane detective John Miller recalls that his blood pressure rose and his weight increased significantly. "I became so obsessed I never slept a full night,"[17] he remembers.

Instead of feeling good about their personal sacrifices, most members battle guilt that comes from neglecting their families and other responsibilities. Some go through the turmoil of divorce when a spouse decides the sacrifice is no longer worthwhile. At work, they are faced with coworkers who resent the special attention they receive and the money they drain from other projects. The secrecy they must maintain so the press does not leak their progress to the killer makes them seem aloof and unfriendly.

Pressure to catch the killer is always with them, and it is made worse by the awareness that, despite their skill and best efforts, he or she may never be caught. Or, if the killer is apprehended, it may be because of luck rather than their hard work. Harvey Glatman, who murdered three women in the Los Angeles area in the late 1950s, was tracked by noted serial killer expert Pierce Brooks, yet he was captured by a California highway patrolman who came upon him and a potential victim as

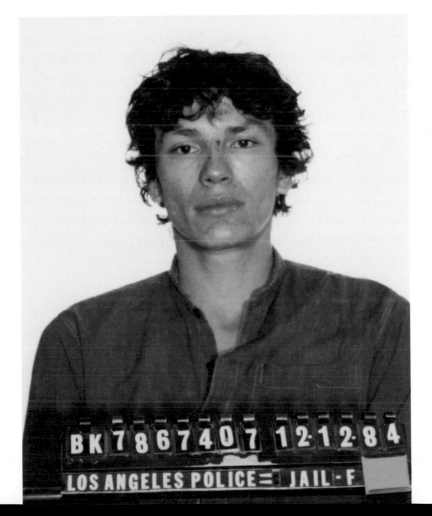

Serial killer Richard Ramirez, the "Night Stalker," was turned in to police by angry neighbors who caught him trying to steal a car.

she struggled to escape. Los Angeles Night Stalker Richard Ramirez, who was wanted for fourteen murders committed in 1985, was turned over to police by angry neighbors who caught him trying to steal a car in the midst of his killing rampage. An off-duty police officer caught Lipstick Murderer William Heirens while he was burglarizing a building. Heirens killed three women in Chicago between 1945 and 1946. At the station house, he signed his name with the same distinctive flourish that characterized a message left in lipstick at one of the murder scenes. The alert officer noticed the similarity, and Heirens's killing spree was over.

To improve their chances of catching murderers like Ramirez and Heirens, modern-day task force members turn to men and women who understand serial killers better than anyone else in law enforcement. These are the profilers, individuals who analyze crimes and the way they are committed to help predict characteristics of an offender who has not yet been identified. Profiling has become extremely popular in recent years. Profilers have their own television shows, write best-selling books, and are often portrayed as the mainstay of the investigation. They are quick to point out, however, that they are simply one of the team, on hand to educate investigators. As Special Agent Mark A. Hilts, chief of the FBI's Behavioral Analysis Unit, states, "We're simply one of the tools in the toolbox. In some cases, we play a bigger role than in others in the resolution of the case. . . . What's appropriate is to address serial killers in a multi-disciplinary way. . . . It's not just a law enforcement problem."[18]

CHAPTER 2

Probing the Minds of Killers

Profiling, also known as criminal investigative analysis or investigative psychology, is a relatively recent addition to a task force's arsenal of weapons. Nevertheless, the technique was used informally in the past. In England, for instance, police surgeon Thomas Bond, who performed an autopsy on one of Jack the Ripper's victims, suggested that the killer was probably quiet and inoffensive looking, but had "great coolness and daring."[19] In America in the 1950s, criminal psychiatrist James Brussel drew up an amazingly accurate profile of George Metesky, who had been setting off bombs around New York City for sixteen years. Brussel described Metesky down to his double-breasted suit. Brussel also provided law enforcement with a profile of the Boston Strangler that closely fit Albert DeSalvo. DeSalvo, a factory worker, confessed to the murder of thirteen women in 1964.

Former agent Howard Teten introduced the FBI to profiling beginning in the 1970s. He writes, "I developed the FBI's original approach to profiling as a lecture course in 1970. . . . The idea was conceived in about 1961–62. However, it was necessary to test the approach using solved cases for about 7 years and to check with several psychiatrists to ensure I was on firm ground . . . before I felt it was ready for presentation."[20]

FBI agents Roy Hazelwood, John Douglas, and Robert K. Ressler modified and popularized Teten's techniques in subsequent years. Today, psychologists, psychiatrists, and other behavioral scientists who have studied crimes and criminals in-depth carry out profiling. These experts are creative thinkers who are able to remain objective and fair-minded even while trying to understand the thinking and reasoning of the most

Criminal psychiatrist James Brussel drew up an astonishingly accurate profile of a serial bomber in the 1950s.

heinous murderers. They examine what those killers do to victims. They spend hours interviewing them in prison. As a result, they have learned how certain behavior predicts a certain type of criminal. As Ressler and coauthor Tom Shachtman explain, "The profiler looks for patterns in crimes and tries to come up with the characteristics of the likely offender. . . . We learn all we can from what has happened, use our experience to fathom the probable reasons why it happened, and from these factors draw a portrait of the perpetrator of the crime."[21]

What Kind of Person?

When it comes to serial killers, a variety of types of profiling are used to help the task force in its hunt. The most common is offender profiling, which focuses on the characteristics of the killer. There is also victim profiling, which analyzes who the killer is targeting and why; crime scene profiling, which involves analysis of the crime scene; and geographical profiling, which helps determine where the killer is likely to be found.

Offender profiling concentrates on elements such as the perpetrator's age, race, background, and motives. Profilers are aware that a "typical" perpetrator is a Caucasian male between the ages of eighteen and thirty-five. He comes from a dysfunctional family and was a victim of physical or sexual abuse. He wet the bed into his teen years, was fascinated with fires, and abused animals at an early age.

Profilers also know that the typical serial killer is intelligent, but he did not do well in school. He was and is perceived

Step by Step: Creating a Criminal Profile

When criminal profilers create a psychological profile of a serial killer, they proceed as follows:

1 Evaluate the criminal act(s).

2 Evaluate the crime scene(s).

3 Analyze the victim(s).

4 Read and evaluate preliminary police reports.

5 Evaluate the medical examiner's autopsy report.

6 Develop a profile of the offender's characteristics.

7 Suggest future investigation based on that profile.

Ted Bundy is considered by many profilers to be the prime example of a psychopath: charming, good-looking, self-centered, remorseless, and highly manipulative.

as pleasant, but he has no close friends. Rather, he has a rich fantasy life in which he is all-controlling. His fantasies have a strong sexual aspect, often involving domination, submission, and murder. These fantasies dominate his thoughts and are the most important thing in his life. Robert D. Keppel and coauthor William J. Birnes write, "Most serial killers have been living with their fantasies for years before they bubble to the surface and are translated into deeds. When the killer finally acts out, some aspect of the murder will demonstrate his unique personal expression that has been replayed in his fantasies over and over again."[22]

Profilers are aware that a typical serial killer is often a psychopath; that is, he has an antisocial personality disorder that is revealed in aggressive, perverted, criminal, or unprincipled behavior. Psychopaths are self-centered, deceptive, emotionally shallow, and feel no guilt or remorse for their actions. They are often attractive, but they are manipulative and chronic liars. Forensic psychologist Stuart Kinner notes, "Probably the pin-up boy for psychopathic people is Ted Bundy. . . . He's clearly a very charming guy, clearly a very remorseless guy, and clearly a very manipulative guy."[23]

Despite their ability to predict what the typical killer will be like, profilers always keep in mind that there are many exceptions to the norm. Atlanta Child Killer Wayne Williams was black, not Caucasian. Aileen Wuornos was female. Gary Ridgway had an IQ of only eighty-two, when one hundred is average. Spokane killer Robert Yates Jr. came from a loving home. Thus, profilers caution that their analyses will seldom be perfect. Overall, however, they can be accurate enough so that law enforcement has some idea of the kind of person for whom they should be looking.

Killer Motives

While it is fairly easy to predict the age, race, and intelligence of unknown killers, profilers know that their motives are more varied and complex. There are killers who like to think they are ridding the world of unworthy people, for instance. They tell themselves they are doing society a favor by murdering prostitutes, homosexuals, or people of a certain ethnic background. John Wayne Gacy, who killed thirty-three young men in Chicago between 1972 and 1978, claimed to kill for this

Herbert Mullin's mental illness caused him to obey a voice that directed him to kill thirteen people in order to prevent a massive earthquake.

reason. So did the so-called Zebra Murderers, Larry Green, J.C.X. Simon, Manuel Moore, and Jessie Lee Cooke. Part of a black extremist group in San Francisco in the mid-1970s, the four maintained they were earning their way to heaven by killing as many Caucasians as possible. Their fifteen victims ranged from college students to janitors. Some were shot, but others were raped and tortured before being decapitated.

Some serial killers commit murder as a result of mental illness. They claim to hear the voice of God, Satan, or a dead family member who demands that they kill for some reason. For instance, Herbert Mullin, who took the lives of thirteen people between 1972 and 1973, obeyed a voice that directed him to kill to prevent a catastrophic earthquake.

David Berkowitz claimed he killed in obedience to the devil, who spoke to him through his next-door neighbor's dog.

The acts of mentally ill killers often appear bizarre and irrational to outsiders, but they make sense in the context of their disordered thinking. Wisconsin native Edward Gein, who murdered at least two and probably more people beginning in 1954, believed that he was preserving his dead mother's soul inside his body by killing women who looked like her and eating their flesh. Gein's mental deviance inspired a novel and the Alfred Hitchcock thriller *Psycho,* a movie about a disturbed young man dominated by his dead mother. The Vampire of Sacramento, Richard Trenton Chase, killed six people in 1977 and 1978 because he believed his blood was turning into powder. Only by drinking his victims' blood could he replenish his own and ward off death.

Unlike other types of serial killers, mentally ill individuals are relatively easy for law enforcement to identify. They attract attention to themselves because they appear abnormal, often long-haired, thin, and unkempt. After a kill, they may do little to conceal the fact, even appearing in public with blood on their clothes. When police arrested Chase outside his apartment, for instance, his jacket and shoes were bloodstained, and he was carrying a bloodstained gun and a box that held bloody rags and pieces of paper.

Power and Control

Most serial killers are not mentally ill. Rather, they kill because they choose to, and they are motivated by their desire for power and control. This desire stems from the fact that they feel overlooked, powerless, and unappreciated. They perceive others as constantly taking advantage of them. Their acts of violence are a form of revenge and make them feel superior. As they kill, they hold the power of life and death in their hands.

Coupled with their need for power and control, many serial killers are also driven by sadism (taking pleasure from another's pain) and distorted sexual desires. The BTK strangler, for instance, got great sexual pleasure from torturing his victims. He strangled them slowly, choosing the very moment when he wanted them to die. Hurting his victims also sexually stimulated the I-40 Killer, Steven B. Pennell, an electrician who killed five women in Delaware in 1987 and 1988. He exhibited what profilers term *overkill*—beating, strangling, and stabbing his victims in the course of his attacks.

Profilers recognize such emotions—and others—from the way the killer operates and the clues he leaves at the crime

BTK killer Dennis Rader derived sexual pleasure from torturing his victims.

scene. For instance, a perpetrator who mutilates the body after death and places it in a humiliating position is expressing rage. A killer who takes great risks is arrogant and sees him- or herself as invulnerable. Jerry Brudos fell into the latter category, several times snatching victims from parking garages in broad daylight. Ann Rule describes his attitude even after he had been arrested for five murders: "Jerry considered himself brilliant. . . . He did not believe there was a cop in the country who could outsmart him, and he looked forward to the jousting that would take place in the coming interviews, confident that he would win."[24]

Symbols and Stereotypes

In addition to studying offenders such as Brudos, profilers focus on victims because they give additional insight into the movements, motives, intent, and fantasies that drive the perpetrator to kill. Profilers know that when they understand why certain victims were chosen, they can better predict the risks a killer is comfortable taking, his sexual preferences, and his attitude toward the group that the victims represent.

Victims usually fit stereotypes that have symbolic meaning for the killer. They may represent a class of women who the killer believes has rejected him and made him feel stupid all his life. They may be homosexual men to whom the killer is attracted but has been taught are evil. They may represent mother figures whom he both loves and resents. Whatever the case, when studying victims, profilers first note characteristics such as appearance, occupation, personal lifestyle, and last-known activities. These facts give clues to the killer's fantasies and his motives for killing.

If possible, profilers also map victims' movements just before they were murdered in order to find out where they crossed

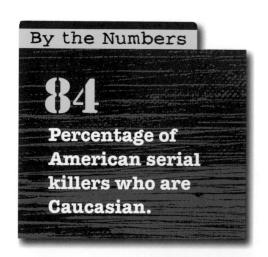

By the Numbers

84

Percentage of American serial killers who are Caucasian.

Jeffrey Dahmer met many of his victims in the gay bars and bathhouses he frequented in Milwaukee.

paths with the killer. They might have shopped in a mall in his neighborhood or gone for drinks in a bar where he spent his evenings. Jeffrey Dahmer met many of his victims in gay bars and bathhouses he frequented in Milwaukee. Dahmer was arrested in 1991 and charged with the murders of fifteen men and boys. The so-called Clairemont Killer, Cleophus Prince, who took the lives of six women in San Diego in 1990, stalked his victims home from fitness centers and gyms in his neighborhood.

Organized and Disorganized

Just as victims provide clues to serial killers' fantasies and motives, crime scenes provide insights into how they plan and execute their murders. More specifically, analyzing the site where

On the Job: Becoming a Profiler

Job Description:
Criminal profilers rely on psychology and experience in criminology to create a portrait of an unknown perpetrator. They perform crime scene analyses, read police reports, and research earlier cases for patterns of criminal behavior.

Education:
Aspiring profilers must earn a four-year degree in behavioral science, criminology, sociology, criminal justice, or a related field from an accredited college or university. They must also gain experience in crime prevention and pass the Profiling General Knowledge Exam, which tests their knowledge of forensic science, victimology, crime scene analysis, criminal profiling, expert testimony, and professional ethics.

Personal Qualifications:
An aspiring profiler must have a logical and analytical approach to work, an open mind, highly developed observational skills, and the willingness to try to understand and think like an offender.

Salary:
A criminal profiler can earn a salary that ranges from forty thousand dollars to more than seventy thousand dollars annually.

the victim was actually killed allows profilers to determine whether they should be looking for a disorganized killer, an organized killer, or someone who shows characteristics of both. The latter includes new killers who can be sloppy and awkward at first but gradually improve their techniques and display more planning as they continue their assaults.

Chaotic crime scenes are the trademarks of disorganized killers. This is because they do not take time to plan their crimes; instead, they strike spontaneously. Restraints arc seldom used because they do not think ahead to bring them along. Blood is likely to be everywhere, and there will be little or no attempt to clean it up. Victims will be left in place. The murder weapon—usually one that is taken from the victim's home—may be left behind, too.

From a chaotic crime scene, profilers know that they are likely looking for a killer who is unintelligent, socially immature, impulsive, and a poor planner. If he works, it is at an unskilled job. His social life will be almost nonexistent. He may drink or use drugs. There is also the possibility that he is

The dirty and disordered kitchen of serial killer Ed Gein demonstrates the mental illness that drove him to kill.

Childhood Influences

Profilers have learned that killers fall into two different categories—organized and disorganized—based on personality and childhood environment.

Organized Killer:
- May be first or only child.
- Father has steady and stable employment.
- Discipline at home is inconsistent.
- Is likely to be disruptive; expresses hurt, anger, and pain.
- May be a bully or a troublemaker.
- Is likely to be very intelligent.
- May be good at schoolwork, but never finishes school.

Disorganized Killer:
- Father's job is unstable.
- Family has problems with drugs, alcohol, and mental illness.
- Discipline at home is harsh.
- Does not express hurt, anger, and pain.
- May be of low intelligence.
- Does not do well at school and will not finish.

seriously mentally ill. If so, he will likely be unemployed, have no car, and will probably live within walking distance of the crime scene. His home will be dirty and will contain evidence of his crimes. When authorities entered Edward Gein's home, for instance, they found a body hanging from the ceiling and body parts scattered throughout the house. Richard Chase's home was just as bad, as forensic psychologist Katherine Ramsland describes: "Nearly everything was bloodstained, including food and drinking glasses. In the kitchen, they found several small pieces of bone, and some dishes in the refrigerator with body parts. One container held human brain tissue. An electric blender was badly stained and smelled of rot."[25]

Organized killers, on the other hand, are much more neat and orderly. They plan their crimes in advance and generally bring along a "killing kit" containing everything they will use in the assault: tape, rope, knives, plastic bags, etc. After the kill, they will take away any weapon and restraints they use. They often move the body from the site of the kill and place it somewhere they have chosen ahead of time.

When the body is left, they will likely pose it in a specific way that satisfies their fantasy.

Whereas disorganized killers attack their victims fast and furiously, organized killers often prolong their murders in order to get the most pleasure from them. Even before a murder, they like to get to know their victims so they can savor the thought of killing them. Then, directly before the kill, they lure the victim into a situation where he or she is powerless. Jerry Brudos took his victims into his garage, which he kept locked and allowed no one to enter. John Wayne Gacy and Jeffrey Dahmer took their victims to their homes and killed them there.

Signatures

As profilers analyze crime scenes, they look for signs that tell them if there is a link between two or more murders. This is often determined by a "signature" that the killer leaves behind. The signature is not the killer's method of operating, such as the fact that he always strikes at night, enters through an open window, or uses a blunt instrument. Rather, the signature is a part of his fantasy, a personal gesture that he feels compelled to leave in order to be satisfied. Keppel and Birnes note, "Signatures [are] a clue not only to what the murderer does, but what he wants, what he seeks, and what drives him from victim to victim. . . . Signatures are the only ways the killer truly expresses himself. . . . If you're smart, you can figure out what the killer is really after."[26]

Not all serial killers leave signatures at the crime scene. When they do, however, they may be obvious, such as staging a corpse in a particular way, tying a victim's bonds in a complicated knot, or leaving messages written in blood. Sometimes the signature is more subtle, however, and experts have to be perceptive to identify it because details can differ from killing to killing. For instance, a killer might cover the head of one victim, leave one victim face down, and place the third in a closet. An expert profiler will see that the signature is the same:

The killer always placed his victims in defeated, submissive positions.

Authorities sometimes have trouble determining if they are looking at a signature or a method of operating. In Spokane's serial murder case, plastic bags were placed over each victim's head. Task force agents debated whether the bags were an expression of the killer's fantasies or were simply his way of staying clean. They finally settled on the latter explanation, particularly as he began using more bags as he continued to kill. Nevertheless, when Spokane detectives came across a victim with a bag over her head, they knew they were looking at the work of their serial killer.

Geographic Profiling

When combined with information obtained from the victim and the crime scene, geographic profiling—determining where the killer lives in relation to his abductions, crime scenes, dump sites, etc.—is important, too. The concept is based on the fact that everyone has a mental map, an image of one's surroundings, that develops as a result of personal experiences, travel routes, reference points, and centers of activity. People are most comfortable within the boundary of their mental map, so profilers postulate that serial killers are most likely to hunt, attack, and dump victims within those boundaries as well.

Creating a geographic profile involves a thorough study of the crimes the killer is believed to have committed. With each crime, investigators gather more data for analysis. In their study, profilers not only examine the crime scenes, but they study evidence as well. They look at area maps and visit the neighborhoods around the scenes. They note details such as the fact that the area where a weapon was found is secluded, that a home that was entered was isolated, or that a victim's body was deposited in an area where other trash abounds. They also note barriers such as bodies of water, high walls, or steep hillsides that might have caused the killer to avoid one route and take another.

Analysis of the information is often carried out on the computer. Computers have made geographic profiling quicker and easier than in earlier times when wall maps and push pins marked the movements of killers. Using one of several software programs specially designed for the purpose, profilers can generate a two- or three-dimensional map showing where crimes and other events occurred. Different colors on the map indicate the statistical probabilities assigned to each section. Red indicates the "jeopardy surface," or the most likely area to find the killer's home, commonly in the geographic center of

A map of the Son of Sam attacks helped investigators create a geographic profile of the killer.

most of the assaults. When the jeopardy surface is pinpointed, the police can investigate further by watching the neighborhood or asking residents to provide information.

Geographic profiling is useful because it can help investigators narrow the area in which they need to search for the killer. It also can help prioritize suspects and cut the amount of time and resources necessary to carry out the investigation. Inspector Glenn Woods of the Royal Canadian Mounted Police says, "Geographic profiling enables you to focus the investigation in a small area of the community rather than on the whole metropolitan area."[27]

Geographic profiling led investigators to within thirteen blocks of Robert Lee Yates Jr.'s home in 1999.

"It's a Guide"

Geographic profiling proved its value when it guided investigators to the neighborhood of serial killer Robert Yates Jr. in Spokane in 1999. The task force was motivated to do a geographic profile because of the logos on the grocery bags on the victims' heads. They postulated that the killer had used bags that had come from stores in his neighborhood. The bags were printed with logos from Albertsons and Safeway, which were plentiful in the Spokane area. One bag was from a Super 1 Foods store, however, and there was only one outlet in Spokane County. That store was located in Spokane's residential South Hill. A little investigation proved that an Albertsons and a Safeway lay within 1 mile (1.6km) of that store as well.

After plotting the locations where the killer dumped his victims as well as the locations of the stores and other key data, the task force came up with general coordinates within which the killer was likely to live. After they had arrested Yates, they were gratified to realize how accurate their profile had been. Spokane sheriff sergeant Calvin Walker states, "Geographic profiling led investigators to within thirteen blocks of Yates' home four months before he was even a suspect. [It helped] us prioritize persons of interest by giving special attention to those living on the South Hill."[28]

Experts are quick to point out that geographic profiling works best when combined with other types of profiling. "When they are applied together, the power of each becomes greater,"[29] says Vancouver police detective Kim Rossmo, a pioneer in the science. Yet even when all types are combined, they are not likely to give a task force the name of a killer or convince a jury that a suspect is guilty. This is because profiling is simply educated guessing based on probabilities and the profilers' experience. As profiler Pat Brown states:

> At this stage, criminal or behavioral profiling is considered more an art than a science. . . . Assuming that human behavior tends to show commonalities, it can seem to be uncannily [amazingly] accurate. But it can also go wrong and sometimes . . . is no help at all. . . . It's a guide. . . . The totality of details are not intended, and should not be taken, as gospel.[30]

CHAPTER 3

Getting the Word Out

The public is the most unpredictable resource a task force draws on in its pursuit of serial killers. Investigators who go public with facts of the case gamble that the more information is circulated, the greater the chance that someone will step forward and provide the clue that brings the monster hunt to an end. At the same time, every investigator knows that publicity has its hazards, including public panic, media criticism, leaks of important information, and more killings. Author and crime expert Marilyn Bardsley observes:

> The demands of the citizens to know what is happening is balanced against the reality that feeding these demands for information virtually ensures that the killer will keep on killing. Legitimate police work is seriously hampered by a deluge of bogus tips from well-meaning citizens. The only party that benefits from this common problem is the media.[31]

Media Cooperation

Because the media is a visible and influential part of the community, it can be an enormous help to task force members. Serial killers sometimes communicate with television or newspaper reporters rather than directly with the task force. When such communications are passed on to investigators, they can provide valuable clues to the killers' thinking, speaking skills, writing style, level of education, and motivations. Between 1968 and 1969, the *San Francisco Chronicle* and the *Vallejo Times-Herald* newspapers shared with police a total of twenty-one cards and letters they received from the so-called Zodiac Killer, who had murdered at least five people in the San Francisco Bay Area beginning in 1966. In addition to clues, the letters held fingerprints and gave details of the murders that investigators did not know. Despite that information, however, the killer was never identified.

In New York City in 1976, journalist Jimmy Breslin received a letter from Son of Sam, who was terrorizing the city at the time. The letter revealed the killer's future plans and held partial fingerprints on its surface. Breslin turned it over to police, and it helped convict David Berkowitz, who was arrested in 1977 in connection with the six killings.

In addition to sharing information, the media can also help investigators by temporarily concealing information they have that could compromise a case. They might withhold their

Two California newspapers shared with police handwritten notes sent to them by the Zodiac Killer.

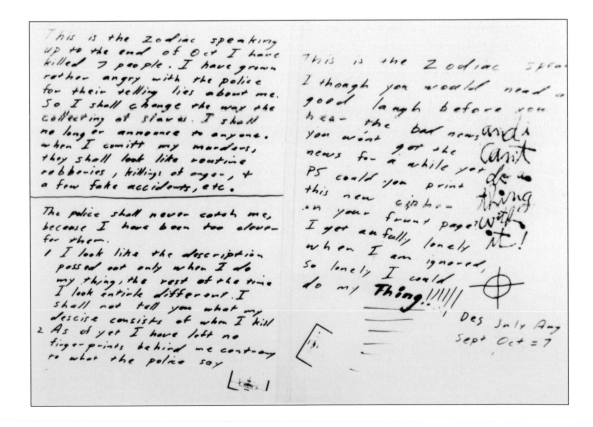

49

knowledge of a unique signature or symbol that the killer leaves. The BTK strangler made his signature—consisting of letters— unique by writing the initials *BTK* horizontally, turning the *B* into a pair of breasts. The press suppressed the information for fear that copycats looking for attention or wanting to cause confusion would send similarly signed messages. Investigators

Serial Killers and the Media

The press and the public are fascinated by serial killers, even though some experts believe that reporting their crimes strokes their egos and leads them to take more lives. Author Morgan Summerfield explains the attraction in an online article entitled "Serial Killer vs. Media: A Symbiotic Relationship?":

Serial killers, to know them is to love them? So it would seem in terms of the media. Once a new serial killer leaps onto the scene with all his or her grisly artistry, the names are burned into our brains by the media. There is intense coverage and sensationalization of their crimes. Do you remember their names? Gacy, Dahmer, Bundy, Son of Sam, the Boston Strangler and the ever popular Jack The Ripper take billing right up there with the Beatles, Pearl Jam, Pink and Good Charlotte as cultural icons. . . . They achieve their place in the annals of history's infamous because the average person is so horrified by what they hear, read or see about them that they must be classified as 'freak.' People do not want to believe that the 'guy or girl next door' might not be what they seem. But, just as with a traffic accident, we can't seem to look away.

Morgan Summerfield, "Serial Killer vs. Media: A Symbiotic Relationship?" www. associatedcontent.com/article/16264/serial_killer_vs_media_a_symbiotic.html.

then could no longer be certain when they saw the symbol that they were looking at the killer's work.

The media also conceals minute but significant details that police may want to keep hidden from the general public. If revealed by a suspect, such details will again identify him as the killer. The information could be about an object always left on the victims' bodies or something that is always taken away. It could be the fact that the arm of one of the victims was broken in the assault. It

By the Numbers

76

Percentage of the world's serial killers who come from the United States.

could be that the killer always cuts his victims' fingernails. In the case of Jerry Brudos, the public was not told that one of the young women killed had been found wearing a loose-fitting, longline (with the band that runs around the torso under the bust extending down to the waist) black bra when she was found, not her own white cotton one. When Brudos mentioned that fact to investigators during questioning, they knew he had been the one to dress her in that garment after he killed her.

Convincing the press to withhold information from the public can be difficult. Often an agreement can be reached only if the argument is made that publishing all the details of the crime will alert the killer to the fact that the task force is closing in. Such was the case when KLXY-TV reporter Cyndy Koures in Spokane discovered that the task force had found the serial killer's DNA on the victims, although they had not yet matched the genetic material to a name. Investigators pointed out that, if the fact was published, the killer could change his method of operating, move to another region, or go into hiding until the excitement died down. Koures agreed not to mention the DNA. "I didn't feel that the public would have benefited from that information. I asked myself, 'Is it worth this one line in this story to possibly damage or jeopardize their investigation?'"[32]

Speculation and Leaks

Despite success in getting the press to cooperate in Spokane, other task force members have found it impossible to convince reporters to keep the details of an investigation hidden. This is because the press believes the public deserves to know what is going on in its community. In addition, murder is always newsworthy, and it draws audiences and sells papers. So even the simple announcement that a task force has been formed will make headlines. "Media attention changes tenfold as soon as you say 'task force.' It changes the way you do business."[33] says Spokane sheriff's lieutenant Douglas Silver, who sometimes spent up to four hours answering the press's questions in the Yates investigation.

When the press gets the story, investigators must deal with reporters' enthusiasm to get more facts, too. This can seriously compromise the case as the reporters go out on the streets or visit victims' families looking for witnesses, conducting interviews, and following leads. Often reporters talk to people even before the police can interview them. In so doing, they discover and broadcast facts that the task force may want concealed. Reporters also wonder and theorize about what they hear and then ask interviewees to comment on the possibilities.

Rumors spread as a result, with some of the guesswork taken as fact. Investigators sometimes learn that witnesses' memories are influenced and their testimony contaminated by press interviews. For instance, in the Green River case, the *Seattle Times* newspaper reported that the first prostitutes to be murdered might have known each other. Shortly after that, informants were telling the police that they had heard that all the victims knew each other. Task force members could not be sure the information was accurate because they did not know if their informants had gotten it from the *Seattle Times* or from their own knowledge. Authors Carlton Smith and Tomas Guillen write, "The trick [for police] was to figure out who really knew something and who didn't, and the uncontrolled publicity was making that task extremely difficult."[34]

Los Angeles Police Chief Daryl Gates talks with the media about a new development in the Hillside Strangler case.

To try to minimize leaks and guesswork, many task forces designate a spokesperson to give out accurate information in a timely way. Spokespersons have to be able to stand up under intense questioning, however, even when there is little news to pass on. They must be aware of their every word and gesture because the press is likely to listen for subtle hints and watch their body language, then report what they think it means. If a spokesperson smiles and appears relaxed, reporters think a break in the case might be coming. If he is sober, they guess that investigators are discouraged.

Even a cautious statement can be blown out of proportion. For instance, in the Green River case, task force commander Frank Adamson was caught off guard when asked by a reporter what he foresaw happening in the case that coming year. Because fewer bodies had been found in recent months, Adamson replied, "By this time next year I'm fairly optimistic we will have him in jail. I'm being optimistic about 1986. I feel good about this year."[35] The following day the *Seattle Times* newspaper bannered his prediction, raising the hopes of city leaders and increasing pressure on the task force for a quick end to the case.

Criticism

An eager press irritates task force members, but they prefer it to criticism that often develops as time passes. Sometimes, of course, the criticism is justified. The press was justly censorious when it discovered that police had talked to Jeffrey Dahmer and one of his young victims less than one hour before the victim's death. The young man, who had been drugged, had been released back into Dahmer's care. The Spokane press was also justifiably critical when it learned that an error in a police report caused task force members, who were investigating owners of white Corvettes, to miss the fact that Robert Yates Jr. drove such a car. If the mistake had not occurred, the case might have been solved three years sooner and several lives could have been saved.

Most of the time, task force members feel that press criticism is unwarranted, however, especially if they end up catch-

The task force working on the Boston Strangler case attracted heavy criticism from the press for its mistakes. Here, Attorney General Elliott Richardson (center, hand raised) and the two officers who took Albert DeSalvo into custody for the murders discuss his capture with the media.

ing the killer. In the Boston Strangler case, the task force was continually charged with inefficiency, and two reporters, Jean Cole and Loretta McLaughlin, made a point of exposing its every mistake, even though it netted Albert DeSalvo after only two years. Likewise, Green River task force members were regularly criticized by area newspapers, which questioned their skills and downplayed the progress they made.

The Baton Rouge Multi-Agency Task Force came under criticism as it tracked Derrick Todd Lee in 2003, although members tried to be flexible in their approach. They ran informational billboard advertisements, took DNA samples from at least one thousand individuals, released details of the case to invite tips, and investigated numerous men with suspicious backgrounds. Former FBI profiler Gregg McCrary observes that fault finding is almost inevitable in such cases: "Whether you capture a killer after 11 homicides or after two, it's never quickly enough. Those who criticize the most typically have the least appreciation for the daunting complexity of this type of investigation."[36]

Investigators are particularly sensitive to press criticism because they realize that negative publicity eventually undermines public support. Then interest wanes, and as other societal problems arise, city and state officials withdraw financial support. In both the Green River Killer case and the Yates case in Spokane, funds set aside for the investigation were cut as time passed and other priorities arose. All five participating members of the Spokane Police Department were pulled from the latter case in December 1999 due to budget cuts. The reductions were a serious threat to progress. Spokane County sheriff Mark Sterk later remarked, "The task force's major complaint was a lack of resources. They needed forensic work done, as well as new computers and an experienced crime analyst, a position for which they never received funding. The most difficult time was when

The Stages in a Serial Murder

Serial killers progress through most of the following stages before and during each of their assaults. The more stages that are present, the more organized, intelligent, and successful the killer is likely to be.

1 Fantasy: The offender is motivated by an idea, thought pattern, or desire.

2 Stalking: The offender follows the victim until the time appears right for the attack. During this time, the victim is depersonalized and becomes nothing more than an object in the killer's mind.

3 Abduction: This phase is not included in a disorganized offender's blitz-style attack. An organized killer uses conversation or some type of deception to get the victim into his or her power.

4 Murder: The act may be decisive and immediate or long and drawn out. It often follows a "script" in the killer's mind, which can include binding, torturing, and mutilation after death.

5 Disposal: The killer may leave the body at the site of the kill, hide it, or move and display it prominently to advertise his or her presence.

county commissioners suggested breaking up the task force and allocating the funds elsewhere."[37]

Partners in Crime Solving

Task force members are aware that, just like politicians and the press, the public can be both helpful and hurtful to a serial killer investigation. On the positive side, the public is essentially the eyes and ears of the task force, which cannot be every place all the time. Truckers on their routes are liable to notice a vehicle parked in a secluded turnout in the dead of night. Prostitutes working the streets know who the threatening men are. Family members can say if a husband and father acts suspiciously or hides sinister activities behind his apparently ordinary exterior. FBI profiler John Douglas observes, "Your greatest partner in solving any crime of violence is the public. Somebody has seen something. Somebody knows something. Undoubtedly many people have seen this perpetrator and looked right through him."[38]

Unless members of the public are informed, however, they do not know who or what to look for. Those who have suspicions keep them to themselves because they do not know exactly what to do or if their information will be helpful. For instance, police learned after arresting John Wayne Gacy that his neighbors had been repelled by a foul odor that hung around his home. They assumed the problem had to do with his drains, not dreaming the smell was caused by decaying bodies that were buried in the crawl space under the house. After BTK strangler Dennis Rader was arrested, investigators discovered that he had been known as a "bureaucratic bully" who frightened some of his neighbors. One woman recalled that he had had her dog put to death without consulting her, simply because it escaped from her yard. Another woman remembered that she had caught him peeking in her windows, and that he had stalked her because he did not like her boyfriend.

In order to motivate the public to share what they know or suspect, authorities hold press conferences and create public service announcements. They ask for help. They give information such as where the killer struck in the past, how many lives he or she has taken, and who is at risk in the future. They show eyewitness sketches of the killer. They publish hotline numbers where information can be called in. They even post rewards and appeal directly to the killer to turn himself in.

The Green River Killer task force used such techniques when it put together the television special "Manhunt Live: A Chance to End the Nightmare," which aired in 1988. Designed to give the struggling investigation new momentum, the program drew 50 million viewers and generated more than fifteen hundred leads. Other task forces have preferred to rely on already existing television shows such as *Unsolved Mysteries* and *America's Most Wanted (AMW)* to draw public attention to their cases. Canadian pig farmer and alleged prostitute-killer Robert Pickton; the Railroad Killer, Angel Maturino Resendez; and the BTK strangler, Dennis Rader, were three serial killers profiled on *AMW*. Alleged serial killer James Allen Kinney, wanted for murders in Michigan, Iowa, Idaho, Oregon, and Washington State, was captured in North Carolina in 2001 when police acted on a tip received after *AMW* featured his crimes.

Task forces investigating serial killers sometimes use television shows like America's Most Wanted *to get leads on their cases. The host of the show, John Walsh, is pictured here.*

Payoff

Over time, serial killers other than Kinney have been caught with the help of the public. In the hunt for Richard Trenton Chase in California, a young woman responded to the published description of the suspected killer and named Chase, her former high school classmate, whom she had just seen at a shopping center. In the Unabomber case, in which an unidentified serial bomber wounded twenty-three people and killed three more over the course of seventeen years, the publishing of his manifesto in the *New York Times* and the *Washington Post* newspapers in 1995 led David Kaczynski to recognize the writing style of his brother Theodore. David Kaczynski remembers, "We shared our suspicions with the FBI agents and helped them investigate and ultimately arrest my brother. Ironically, a 17-year manhunt . . . was powerless to catch the Unabomber . . . until an anguished family came forward, willing to turn over a loved one because it recognized its responsibility to protect others."[39]

The BTK strangler case had been unsolved for thirty years when Wichita attorney Robert Beattie realized that many of the students in the political science class he was teaching were unaware that the killer was still at large. In 2003 he began writing a book about the case and was prominently featured in the local media. In 2004 the publicity caused the killer—who had written taunting letters to the police and newspapers before— to break his sixteen-year silence and send a letter to the *Wichita Eagle* newspaper. Further communication followed, and with new evidence to go on, authorities made an arrest in February 2005. Former Wichita police chief Floyd B. Hannon Jr., who had hunted BTK from 1974 until 1976, said to Beattie in 2005, "Without your interest in writing a book and . . . also causing the person who committed the crimes to start showing off, this case might still not be solved. For this I thank you."[40]

Bizarre and Incredible

Members of the public can be an enormous help in a serial murder investigation, but, like the media, they can also cause

Police caught Unabomber Ted Kaczynski with the help of his brother David Kacyznski (shown right, escorting his mother Wanda Kaczynski to the courthouse).

complications. Sometimes they panic when they hear the news that a serial killer is on the loose. Like Wichita residents who boarded their windows and purchased guns in the BTK strangler case in the 1980s, Los Angeles residents lived in fear when the Hillside Strangler was claiming victims in the late 1970s. Sales of burglar alarms skyrocketed. Many women took self-defense classes and walked in pairs, especially after dark. Men purchased revolvers, switchblade knives, and baseball bats to arm their wives and girlfriends.

Even when the public does not panic, results of the publicity—usually thousands of tips and suggestions—can overwhelm investigators. Many of these submissions are bizarre, incredible, and a waste of the task force's time. During the Green River Killer investigation, for instance, an amateur detective from Tacoma insisted that the killer was simply a robber intent on stealing prostitutes' jewelry. He urged investigators to stake out pawnshops if they wanted to catch him. In the Yates case in Spokane, a tipster suggested the task force place a department store mannequin on a street corner and wait for the killer to attack it. Spokane sheriff sergeant Calvin Walker says, "Do you discard this stuff? No. But you give it the weight it appears to have."[41]

While unlikely suggestions may be ignored, many tips warrant investigation. Men who have reportedly committed violent acts have to be checked out and eliminated. So do those who act suspiciously, such as several dozen Los Angeles men who impersonated police officers and frightened women at the

Nicknames for Serial Killers

To give punch to their stories, members of the media like to tag serial killers with catchy nicknames. The following are examples:

- Want-Ad Killer Harvey Carignan—killed young women, at least one of whom had answered his help-wanted advertisement in the newspaper.
- Trash Bag Killer Patrick Kearney—wrapped his victims neatly in trash bags.
- Candy Man Dean Corll—worked in his mother's candy factory and generously handed out candy to children; later went on to murder at least twenty-seven boys and young men.
- Stocking Strangler Gary Carlton—also nicknamed the Chattahoochee Choker, he strangled elderly women with their own stockings, which he left knotted around their necks.
- Score-Card Killer Randy Kraft—kept a coded notebook with a tally of the young men he murdered.
- I-5 Killer Randall Woodfield—traveled up and down Interstate 5, choosing victims in Washington, Oregon, and California.
- Sunday Morning Slasher Coral Watts—enjoyed killing women on Sunday morning before he went to church.

time of the Hillside Strangler case. The tips also raised the possibility that someone in law enforcement could be the perpetrator. Task force members took the time to investigate each other simply to eliminate the slim possibility that the killer was in their midst. A similar internal investigation took place in the BTK case, when task force members were asked to give a DNA sample in order to be positively ruled out as suspects. "We are collecting swabs to eliminate with certainty, personnel who were employed during the time period in which the BTK murders occurred,"[42] explained Lieutenant Kenneth Landwehr, who headed the investigation in 2004.

BTK investigators learned by experience that even the most credible tips need a thorough follow-up. In 1979 a respectable middle-aged woman who lived with her husband in Wichita came forward, claiming that she was being harassed and stalked by BTK. She not only produced letters and poems that he had allegedly mailed to her, but she also had to be rushed to the hospital after the killer apparently assaulted her and stabbed her in the back. For three years, members of the task force worked to protect her while using her leads to track the perpetrator. Finally, they became suspicious and determined that the woman had concocted the evidence in order to gain protection from the real killer.

False Confessions

Involving the public in a case not only brings in thousands of tips, but it also triggers false confessions. Some of these confessions come from individuals who are mentally ill. Some are guilt-ridden or full of self-hatred. Some simply want attention. Although all deserve help if they want it, they distract investigators from pursuing more valuable leads.

Investigators in the Boston Strangler case were plagued with suspects who confessed to being the killer. Even today, some people question whether Albert DeSalvo, who admitted to and was convicted of the crimes, was not one of the false confessors. In the Green River Killer case, serial killer Henry

Lee Lucas, in prison in Texas, told authorities that he had committed the murders in Washington State. Although Lucas was guilty of other killings, investigators who interviewed him eventually determined that he had not been in the Pacific Northwest at the time of the Green River assaults. As part of the Yates case, investigators flew to South Dakota in response to information that a resident of that state was bragging that he had killed prostitutes in Spokane. An interview and a blood sample were enough to prove that the man was lying.

Increasingly, investigators are relying on blood analysis rather than confessions and eyewitness testimony to determine whether they have a perpetrator correctly matched to a series of crimes. Such analysis, carried out in crime labs across the country, is slow and methodical and does not rate the attention that a profiler or a police spokesperson gets. Nevertheless, it is through lab analysis that many of the mysteries of the case are solved. Author and commentator Stanley Crouch writes, "The crime lab [analysts] have the very important job of measuring and evaluating. What they bring forward can lead to putting an unmoving collar around the neck of a killer who may have gone on to live a very new life after snuffing out someone else's."[43]

Serial killer Henry Lee Lucas confessed to the Green River killings, but investigators determined that he was not in the area at the time of the murders.

CHAPTER 4

Relying on Science

While profilers, the public, and the press make important contributions to serial killing investigations, crime lab experts are the backbone of the case. Their analysis of evidence such as hairs, fibers, fingerprints, and biological material is usually necessary to convict the killer when he or she comes to trial.

Hundreds of crime lab experts work in more than three hundred crime labs throughout the United States. Many of these labs are funded by the federal government. Others are state, county, or city facilities. A growing number are filled with state-of-the-art equipment that includes computers, electron microscopes, and lasers. No matter what the size or status of the lab, the men and women who work in them are usually overwhelmed with evidence to process when a serial murder case is ongoing. Sheriff's aide Shelly Sutton described conditions at the Washington State crime lab during the Green River case in 1985: "The backlog of requests [for analysis] stands at 123. . . . It is important to note that a single lab request may contain hundreds of items of evidence. For example, some of the lab requests are 12 pages long, with ten or more items listed on one page."[44]

Scoping Out Evidence

After evidence found at the crime scene is photographed, logged, and transported to the lab, analysts begin their work by focusing on the most easily lost or destroyed material. Much of this evidence is trace evidence, meaning it is small, often microscopic items such as hair, fibers, metal filings, pollen, or cosmetics. Great care is always taken while working with trace evidence, because a careless movement or a breeze from an air vent can cause something like a chip of paint or a particle of dirt to be blown away and lost.

Analysts rely on a variety of microscopes when scrutinizing trace evidence. In addition to a traditional compound scope, which uses light reflected and magnified through a series of lenses, they utilize comparison scopes, which consist of two microscopes joined by a common eyepiece. Under such scopes, two objects can be viewed at the same time, and differences and similarities can be easily noted. Analysts also use stereoscopic microscopes, which have double eyepieces and double lens systems to better scrutinize three-dimensional images. Electron microscopes, which are found in the best-equipped labs, are invaluable for examining odd-shaped evidence. These scopes utilize a beam of highly energized electrons (subatomic particles) to magnify objects up to one hundred thousand times, thus revealing their structure, composition, and surface features.

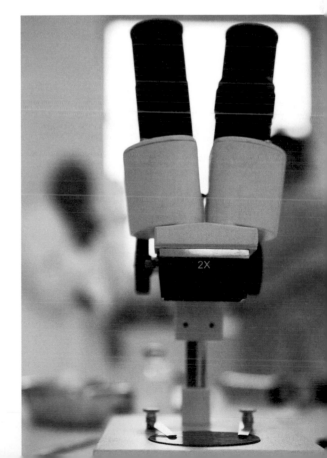

Microscopes such as this one are important tools for investigators in analyzing trace evidence.

Forensic microscopist Skip Palenik relied on the infrared microscope in his lab when he was asked to analyze tiny paint specks found on victims during the Green River Killer investigation. Infrared scopes work with the aid of photoelectric cells to measure the light absorption of evidence that may be no larger than a micron (one-millionth of a meter, or .00004 inches) in size. Palenik, who was able to match the specks with paint found on Gary Ridgway's work coveralls, concluded, "Most of the samples turned out to be made of Imron paint, a very rare type that was used extensively in the paint shop where Ridgway worked at

Kenworth Trucks. Working with Dupont, who manufactured the paint, we were able to tie the samples to paint that Ridgway had been using around the time of the murders."[45]

Fiber and Hair

In addition to paint, hair is also examined microscopically so that analysts can tell from its size, shape, color, and texture whether it is animal or human. If it is human, they can determine if it is Caucasian, African, or Asian. Hair found at a crime scene can be compared to hair from a suspect, and if a match is made, investigators know that it is likely that the suspect has been in close proximity to the body.

Hair helped convict the so-called Texas Eyeball Killer, Charles Albright, in 1991. Not only was Albright's hair found on one of his victims, but the victim's hair also was found in Albright's vacuum cleaner and on a blanket in his truck. Albright earned his nickname because he was known to have an abnormal obsession with eyes. In the three murders linked to him, the victims' eyes had been surgically removed.

The rough grass-like appearance of cotton fibers (left) under the microscope help investigators to distinguish them from smooth nylon fibers (right).

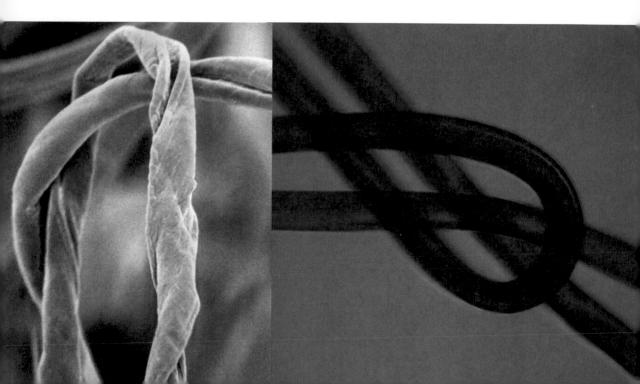

Analysts also microscopically scrutinize fibers found at a crime scene in order to link a killer to his crimes. They first concentrate on shapes. For instance, cotton or flax fibers look like blades of grass under magnification, and nylon or polyester fibers are extremely uniform and smooth. Analysts also look at color, which can be analyzed using a microspectrophotometer, a combination of a microscope and a spectrophotometer (an instrument that helps identify a substance by directing a beam of light at it and ob-

taining what is known as its absorption spectrum). Analysis of twenty-eight different types of fibers that were eventually linked to nineteen items in the home and vehicles of Atlanta Child Killer Wayne Williams helped convict him of his crimes in 1982. Bright blue fibers found on one of several women who were killed in Delaware between 1987 and 1988 led to the arrest of Steven B. Pennell, who owned a van carpeted with such fibers.

Making a Match

In addition to fiber, hair, and paint, trace evidence ranges from plant debris to makeup and gunshot residue. Seen under a microscope, each piece is unique in some way and can often provide clues about the victim, the perpetrator, and the crime.

Plant material played a part in helping bring serial killer Robert Yates Jr. to justice in 2000. The task force on that case noted that three victims had been found partially covered with yard debris, and it postulated that the material could have come from around the killer's home. Botanist Richard Old was asked to analyze the material, and from the mix he identified leaves from Norway maple, honey locust, lace leaf maple, and Eastern white cedar trees. He also found landscaping bark with distinctive diagonal cuts, peanut shells, cherry pits, white paint

On the Job: Becoming a Fingerprint Examiner

Job Description:
Fingerprint examiners analyze evidence in order to determine the presence of fingerprints. They use various physical and chemical techniques as well as instruments such as fuming chambers, alternate light sources, and heat/humidity chambers to make latent prints visible. They are also responsible for analyzing, comparing, and evaluating developed prints in an effort to match them with known recorded fingerprints.

Education:
Aspiring fingerprint examiners must earn a four-year degree in natural science, forensic science, criminology, or a closely related field. They are also encouraged to get at least two years of work experience under the sponsorship of a latent print examiner and become accredited by the National Register of Fingerprint Experts.

Personal Qualifications:
Aspiring fingerprint examiners must be patient, thorough, and willing to pay attention to detail. They should be able to write logical and concise reports and prepare and maintain clear, accurate notes and records.

Salary:
A fingerprint examiner can earn between forty and sixty thousand dollars annually.

chips, and pieces of concrete. Old said, "We ended up with a wonderful picture of what this yard looked like, but we didn't know what it meant."[46]

Investigators discovered the meaning in 2000 after blood from one of the victims was found in Yates's car, and Yates's DNA was matched to DNA found on at least one of the victims. As they searched his home, hoping to find more evidence, Old examined the yard. He found peanut shells and pieces of concrete in one area. He also found all the species of plants that had been in the debris on the victims. Old told investigators, "We've got like 17 species that match. There's nothing in the yard now that doesn't match."[47]

Impressions

Trace evidence such as yard waste is usually not strong enough to stand alone in catching and convicting a killer. It is considered class evidence, which means there are large quantities of it in the world, so it might have originated from another person or place. Experts prefer to rely on individual evidence, which is unique to each human being. Fingerprints, footmarks, bite marks, and other kinds of impressions fall into this category. Criminologist Henry C. Lee emphasizes, "[Fingerprints] constitute the most important category of physical evidence for positive identification or individualization."[48]

When it comes to fingerprints, examining them is a lengthy process because raised ridges that form loops, whorls, and arches on two sets of prints have to be scrutinized and compared to try to get as many matching points as possible (usually a minimum of ten). Only one point of difference in a comparison study will rule out a suspect.

At a crime scene, visible fingerprints are considered a true find because in many cases prints exist but are latent (invisible). Then analysts must try to find them using a variety of chemicals and techniques. Ninhydrin

Mapped here are the identifying characteristics of a fingerprint used to compare one fingerprint to another.

arch
loop*
whorl

bifurcation

ridge end

core

22 minutiae points

The combination of pattern and wear marks on tires can make impressions unique enough to stand as evidence in a criminal trial.

is widely used for making fingerprints visible on paper surfaces. Cyanoacrylate esters, otherwise known as superglues, have proven effective for developing prints on nonporous surfaces. In the Yates case, analysts relied on a technique called vacuum metal deposition, which uses small amounts of gold and zinc dust to look for latent prints on the thin plastic bags covering the victims' heads. Task force member Fred Ruetsch says, "It used to be that you couldn't recover fingerprints from plastic bags, but now scientists have a new hi-tech way to recover [them]."[49] On one of the bags, investigators raised a partial fingerprint and a palm print that were later matched to Yates's.

Lab analysts love to find fingerprints when evidence is being processed, but tire impressions have also helped them catch serial killers. Although tires are produced in great number, the combination of pattern and wear marks acquired during use can make them unique. In the case of Florida murderer Robert "Bobby Joe" Long, investigators quickly noticed that impressions found near one of the victims suggested that the killer had mismatched tires on his car. Molds of the impressions were sent to a tire expert in Ohio. He identified them as having been made by a Goodyear Viva tire and a Vogue Tyre, the latter an expensive brand that was relatively rare. From the size of these tires, the expert also deduced that the suspect was driving a medium- or full-size car. That information matched Long's Dodge

Magnum with mismatched tires and helped prosecutors convict him of nine murders after he was apprehended in 1984.

Bite Marks

Less widely used than fingerprints, bite marks can also be unique enough to help convict a serial killer. A bite mark on human skin is a strong indication of guilt, because bites are not linked with ordinary daily activities.

Investigators often find bite marks in serial murder cases where a female victim has been sexually assaulted and killed. When any semicircular bruise or wound about 2 inches (5.08cm) in diameter is discovered, they call in a forensic odontologist— a specialist who studies the structure, development, and abnormalities of teeth—to perform an examination. He or she uses special lights to bring up details that are invisible under normal white light. Journalist Shannon Rasp writes, "Ultraviolet light

Dr. Richard Souviron, a forensic odontologist, points to a photograph of Ted Bundy's teeth during Bundy's murder trial. The bite marks found on Lisa Levy match Bundy's bite.

Step by Step: Taking Fingerprints

Digital fingerprinting devices are becoming common, but many police departments still rely on paper and ink systems. To record fingerprints accurately, law enforcement officials adhere to the following procedure:

1 Position inking plate or pad approximately 39 inches (.99m) from the floor. If the pad is not at this height, the technician could fail to capture the lower portion of the first joint of the finger, and necessary ridge detail will be missing.

2 Clean and dry subject's fingers.

3 Position subject in front of and at a forearm's length from the pad.

4 Beginning with the right hand, grasp the subject's hand at the base of the thumb with the right hand. The technician's hand should be cupped over the subject's, and those fingers not being printed must be tucked back. Using the left hand, the technician then guides the finger being printed.

5 Roll the bulb of each finger on the inking plate or pad so that the entire fingerprint pattern area is evenly covered with ink. Ink must cover from one edge of the nail to the other and from the crease of the first joint to the tip of the finger. If too little ink is used, the impression will be too light; if too much ink is used, fine details will run together.

6 Place the side of the finger on the paper fingerprint card, and roll the finger to the other side until it faces the opposite direction. Care should be exercised so the bulb of each finger is rolled evenly from tip to below the first joint. Generally the weight of the finger is all the pressure needed to clearly record the fingerprint.

can help law enforcement when it comes to forensic dentistry, illuminating bite marks that are invisible to the naked eye."[50]

Once positively identified, a bite mark can reveal a unique pattern of cuts and bruises that are not easily reproduced by someone else's teeth. Forensic dentist Veronique Delattre explains, "There are 28 teeth, plus four wisdom teeth, in an adult's dentition [set of teeth]. Each tooth has five surfaces. . . . Each surface has its own characteristics and may have fillings, crowns, extractions, bridges, etc."[51] In addition to surface irregularities, teeth can vary in size, spacing, and alignment. Thus, a murderer with crooked teeth will leave a distinctly crooked pattern of bruises on the skin. A person with prominent canine teeth will leave exceptionally large, dark bruises or even lesions where those teeth press. Odontologists investigate a bite by creating a mold of the suspect's upper and lower teeth, then placing that mold over a photo of the wound. If the mold fits the bite mark exactly, it is considered a match.

A bite mark left on the body of twenty-year-old Lisa Levy was key evidence that helped convict serial killer Ted Bundy. Bundy bit his victims both during and after his murders. When the wounds on Levy were compared to an impression of Bundy's teeth, they were shown to be a perfect match. Author Katherine Ramsland writes, "This was the first case in Florida's legal history that relied on bite-mark testimony, and the first time that a physical piece of evidence actually linked Bundy with one of his crimes."[52]

Biological Evidence

Biological evidence has become as important as fingerprints and bite marks when a task force is tracking a serial killer. Biological evidence includes blood, bones, semen, and mucus, and when investigators come across it at a crime scene, they collect it with particular care.

The medical examiner is the first to determine if biological evidence is present when the remains of a victim are found. After supervising the collection of the remains, he or she performs an autopsy, which is a postmortem (after-death) medical examination of the corpse. When biological material such as semen or mucus is found during the autopsy, the medical examiner collects it and sends it to the lab for DNA analysis. DNA, or deoxyribonucleic acid, is genetic material that is unique to each individual and can identify the killer. DNA can also be used to identify a victim because it is present in all cells, including those in bone and in the roots of hair.

The ability of crime lab investigators to use DNA as an identification tool has had a revolutionary effect on bringing killers to justice. After almost twenty years, the Green River task force was able to arrest Gary Ridgway in 2001 when analysts matched his DNA to DNA found on the bodies of four of his victims. In 2003 DNA analysis connected Chester Dewayne Turner to thirteen murders that took place in Los Angeles between 1987 and 1998. Other serial killers arrested due to DNA evidence include Dennis Rader, Robert Yates Jr., John Eric

A coroner prepares an autopsy report. The autopsy often uncovers evidence such as semen or mucus that can be used to identify a killer.

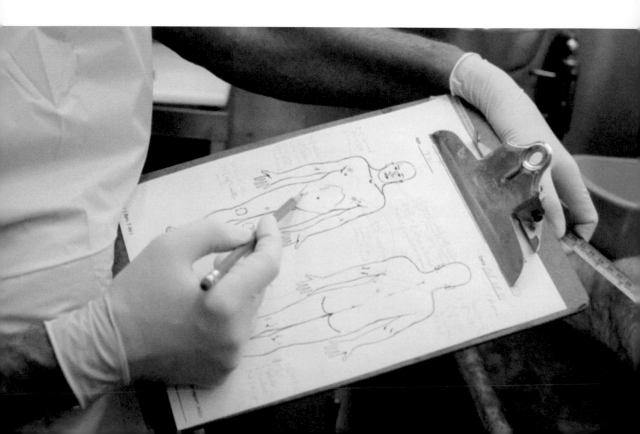

The Limits of DNA Profiling

Even if a forensic anthropologist gets a DNA profile from a victim, identification cannot be made until the profile is matched to a missing person. That often involves luck as well as a great deal of work. The DNA of criminals is regularly kept on file, but there is no DNA database for the general population.

To obtain lists of individuals who might be the victim, investigators generally turn to missing-person files, found in several databases on the Internet. These files give names, dates of birth, race, height, weight, and where the missing person was last seen. Usually there are many possibilities, and investigators end up with a large pile of printouts to evaluate. If a potential match is found, they then contact the agency that submitted the information in hopes of getting DNA, dental records, or other information.

The process can take days or weeks. Making a match brings investigators a great deal of satisfaction. Too often, however, the victim was a loner, a homeless person, or a prostitute who had never been reported missing. Then the case remains unsolved, and the hunt goes on.

Armstrong, Lorenzo Gilyard, and Arhon Kee. Armstrong was arrested by Detroit police for at least five murders in the 1990s. Gilyard is charged with killing thirteen women in Kansas City, Missouri, between 1977 and 1993. Kee killed at least three women in New York City between 1991 and 1998.

While most DNA analysis is carried out with nuclear DNA, there are times when mitochondrial DNA (mtDNA)—DNA found outside the nucleus of a cell—is used to identify murder victims and link killers to crimes. MtDNA is found in mitochondria (structures that provide energy in the cell) and is passed unchanged from a mother to her children. If a suspect or a victim is not available to match to DNA found at a crime scene, mtDNA from a mother or sibling can be assessed for identification purposes.

MtDNA was used to convict serial killer Hadden Clark of the murder of six-year-old Michele Dorr in Maryland in 1999. After bloodstains on the floorboards of his brother's home were found to match DNA samples from Dorr's mother, Clark confessed to stabbing the little girl and later led police to her body. Clark is believed to have killed as many as a dozen women and girls on the East Coast between the mid-1970s and 1993.

Bones

In many serial murder cases, a long period of time passes before victims are found. With nothing but bones left to analyze, forensic anthropologists are often called in to help with identification. Stanley Rhine, professor emeritus in the Department of Anthropology at the University of New Mexico, explains: "In those cases in which soft tissue has been degraded by time, temperature, environment or other external forces, the only tissue remaining more or less intact is bone. The obvious person to call in to evaluate such material is the bone specialist."[53]

A forensic anthropologist can learn a great deal from a human skeleton, even if it is incomplete. He can estimate age by looking at joints. These are more worn in older people than in younger ones. He can also look at the skull for indications of age and race. Sutures (where the bones join) continue to close throughout life, so a smooth skull indicates an older person. Caucasian skulls are relatively elongated; the lower jaw of Negroid skulls juts forward in a trait called prognathism; Mongoloid (Asian and Native American) skulls are round with flat cheekbones. Sex can be determined by looking at pelvic bones, which are lower and wider in women and narrower in men. Height and body type can be estimated by measurements of the long bones in the legs.

Through such observation, forensic anthropologists can usually determine if the remains are likely one of the killer's victims. If a match is possible, DNA analysis can be carried out with good results. Although nuclear DNA is extremely difficult to come by when working with bones, there is usually enough usable mtDNA to create a profile, even if the bones are very old or degraded.

Sometimes an identification can be made without DNA analysis. When Jeffrey Dahmer informed police that his first murder had taken place in 1978 in his hometown of Bath, Ohio, they went in search of evidence to prove this killing. Dahmer had told them that he had killed an eighteen-year-old hitchhiker named Steven Hicks, cut up his body, then later crushed Hicks's bones with a sledgehammer and scattered them in a wooded area near his home. In 1991 the area he indicated was searched and did indeed yield small pieces of human bones. Some were less than .5 inches (1.27cm) long. The largest was just over 2 inches (5.08cm).

Investigators asked Douglas Owsley, an anthropologist at the Smithsonian Institution in Washington, D.C., to examine the bone fragments. In his lab, Owsley discovered that some bore cut marks that supported Dahmer's statement that he had

When a body has decomposed beyond the point of recognition, a forensic anthropologist can still glean information about the victim from the skeletal remains.

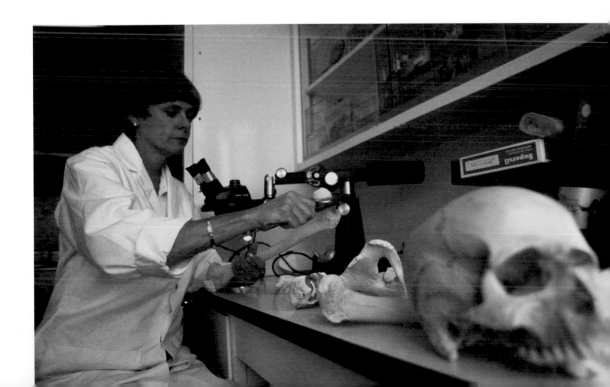

dismembered Hicks. When he pieced the fragments together, Owsley also determined that the bones were male and consistent with Hicks's height and age. Finally, he obtained medical and dental X-rays taken of Hicks before he disappeared and compared them to fragments of teeth and vertebrae that had been recovered. The match was exact, and authorities were able to announce that a positive identification of Hicks had been made.

Even with scientific advances like DNA analysis, serial killers like Jeffrey Dahmer and Hadden Clark got away with murder for years because they killed in a variety of locales, even in different states. In the past, there was no easy way to determine if a missing person in Ohio, for instance, was linked to a murder in Chicago. Investigators had to rely on telephones, the mail, or wire services if they wanted to communicate with each other, and they seldom, if ever, shared files. As Bobby Joe Long bragged in 1992, "All I had to do was throw my stuff in a car and move to Lakeland or Miami or Daytona or out of state and they'd never track me down."[54]

The relatively recent development of computer databases and software programs has made communication easier for law enforcement, however. Some of these programs are fully operational, but others are still being developed. Whereas some are state sponsored, the federal government coordinates others. Everyone who is involved with them, though, believes that they make a significant difference when hunting for killers. Richard "Jack" Hunt, director of federal law enforcement for the GTE Corporation, a commercial database provider, states, "Crime problems now straddle community lines more than ever and we have to battle [them] in new ways. There has always been an informal sharing network, but now technology is allowing us to formalize it and use it more effectively."[55]

CHAPTER 5

High-Tech Tactics

Technology is becoming invaluable in tracking serial killers, and expert Robert D. Keppel was one of the first law enforcement officers to recognize its potential. He turned to the computer to try to identify Ted Bundy in the 1970s, although the system he used was not nearly as fast or as people-friendly as today's personal computers. Keppel remembers:

> There were terminals that were hooked up to a mainframe computer that was the size of a room a couple of hundred feet [61 meters] long and fifty feet [15.2 meters] wide. That computer had belts and punch cards and keypunch operators entering and recording data. . . . We had collected so many names and different lists of information. The computer people told me that they could collate [sort and arrange] that and tell me how many times one person appeared on more than one list. It took about a month to go through the entire process."[56]

Computers have become smaller, faster, and more sophisticated since Keppel hunted Bundy. Task forces can now access a variety of information products and systems, ranging from video imaging tools to DNA databanks, that help them track killers with greater efficiency and less effort.

Specialized Software

Some high-tech programs available to law enforcement today target a specific task. There is software to analyze bloodstain patterns found at crime scenes. There is software that helps experts calculate the trajectories of projectiles like bullets moving through the atmosphere.

Facial identification software contains images and biographical information about criminals from across the United States. Facial reconstruction software can age-progress faces of victims or suspects to help the public more easily identify them. Image overlay programs allow investigators to place a fingerprint, signature, or bullet image over live images in order to make comparisons.

Programs such as Forensic Audio Lab by Visiosonic remove unwanted noise from tape recordings. Muffled, noisy, or barely audible audio surveillance tapes or 911 messages can be transformed into clear recordings that are easily heard and understood. Likewise, the Video Imaging Tool for Aiding Law Enforcement (VITALE), developed by the Oak Ridge

The IBM computers used in the FBI offices in 1967 were not nearly as fast and efficient as the computers available to law enforcement officials today.

National Laboratory in Tennessee, removes unwanted shadows, distortion, or "snow" from videotapes. VITALE chooses samples of multiple frames of surveillance footage of a subject, compiles information on that subject from different views, and then fuses the data together to sharpen the image. The technique enables users to do things like read words on T-shirts and see details of facial features. Laboratory spokesman Ron Walli says, "We believe this new technology will make a significant difference in solving crimes that would perhaps otherwise remain unsolved."[57]

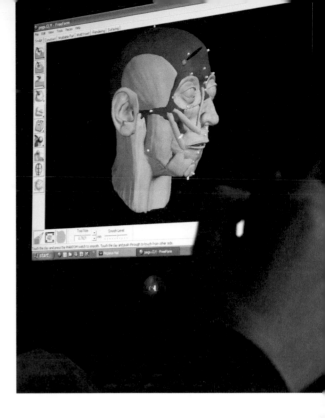

Facial reconstruction programs such as the one shown here are valuable in age-progressing suspects or victims, as well as re-creating a person's likeness from a skull.

Fingerprint Identification Systems

The FBI's Integrated Automated Fingerprint Identification System (IAFIS) is another example of technology that is making a significant difference to task forces and other law enforcement personnel throughout the country. Established in 1999, this national fingerprint and criminal history database is the largest in the world and contains information on more than 47 million individuals. In using it, even the smallest law enforcement agency can have access to the prints of felons throughout the United States, an opportunity they did not have with earlier paper systems.

When a task force wants to identify an unknown fingerprint, it scans it electronically and enters it into the IAFIS system. There, it is digitally encoded into a geometric pattern. It is then compared to other prints in the system, which have been previously submitted by local, state, and federal law enforcement agencies throughout the country. The program comes up with prints that are possible matches, and investigators then make a final point-by-point visual comparison of

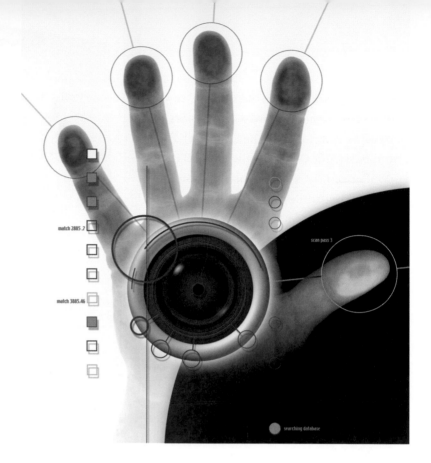

match 2885 .2

match 3885.46

scan pass 3

searching database

The FBI's national fingerprint database provides law enforcement agencies access to felons' fingerprints throughout the United States.

the unknown print with the alternatives. This last step is somewhat slow and tedious, but the process is significantly faster than earlier ones in which the unknown print had to be manually compared to the thousands of prints that an agency had in its paper files.

Police in Los Angeles credit their Automated Fingerprint Identification System (AFIS), one of the predecessors of IAFIS, for aiding in the identification of Richard Ramirez in 1985. A clear fingerprint was found on the back of the rearview mirror on a car that the then-unknown killer had stolen after one of his murderous attacks. That print was entered into the database, and because Ramirez's name was in the system for traffic and illegal drug arrests, investigators made a match.

The Combined DNA Index System

In the late 1980s the realization that DNA could be used to tie criminals to their crimes motivated law enforcement agencies to begin compiling databases similar in ideology to AFIS and IAFIS. In 1990 the FBI created the Combined DNA Index System (CODIS), which tied together fourteen local and state DNA laboratories in an information-sharing service. In 1998 CODIS was expanded to include the federal government's National DNA Index System, and participating labs soon existed in all fifty states plus the District of Columbia and Puerto Rico.

CODIS consists of a forensic index, containing DNA evidence found at crime scenes, and an offender index, holding the DNA profiles of known offenders of sex offenses and other violent crimes. Those profiles are created from blood drawn from an offender and processed in the lab. Forensic labs throughout the United States regularly electronically exchange and compare DNA profiles through CODIS, and as of March 2006 more than thirty-one thousand hits have been made, linking unknown DNA to known offenders.

Forensic labs throughout the United States can now electronically exchange known offenders' DNA profiles thanks to CODIS, the Combined DNA Index System.

Some CODIS hits have involved serial killers. In 2003 Alexander Wayne Watson Jr. was identified as the murderer of at least three women in Maryland between 1986 and 1994. Police found saliva on an unlit cigarette near one of the bodies, submitted the DNA found on it to CODIS, and were given Watson's name. In 2006 CODIS linked Juan Mesa Segundo, a known burglar in the Forth Worth, Texas, area, to the murder of at least three women there. Florida homicide detective John Curcio observes, "Evidence was collected in a lot of old cases—like hairs and cigarettes—that we didn't have the technology to do anything with before. But nowadays, you can take that and do something with a case with these databases. The advances in technology now are amazing."[58]

Broad-Spectrum Databases

In addition to specialized databases such as IAFIS and CODIS, computerized information systems are also available to make connections between the thousands of facts that are always gathered in serial-killing cases. Once technicians input such data, the computer can collate it in a variety of ways with little more than the click of a mouse. Thousands of files are scanned in a matter of minutes, allowing task force members to look for cases where the killer drives a white car, uses a knife as a weapon, and poses the body, for instance, or for cases where the killer operates only in one particular state and cuts the buttons off victims' clothes after he kills them. One such program, the Computer Aided Tracking and Characterization of Homicides (CATCH) system, designed by the Pacific Northwest National Laboratory, is being tested in Washington State. "It's very impressive. CATCH can help us link cases in ways we wouldn't necessarily see,"[59] observes expert Bob LaMoria, program manager of the Washington State Homicide

Investigation Tracking System (HITS). HITS was developed in 1987 by LaMoria, Robert D. Keppel, and Joseph Weis of the University of Washington. Like CATCH, it allows investigators to choose from as many as 250 fields of information, ranging from geographic location of the crimes to absence or presence of clothing on the bodies.

Washington is not the only state to have its own crime database. Florida has the Integrated Criminal History System. New York has its Real Time Crime Center, made up of several computer databases that are accessed centrally to quickly relay information and analysis to detectives in the field. Illinois has the Citizen Law Enforcement Analysis and Reporting system and is planning to implement the Classification System for Serial Criminal Patterns (CSSCP) soon. The CSSCP is the creation of Tom Muscarello, an assistant professor at DePaul University in Chicago, and will operate twenty-four hours a day, seven days a week searching for patterns or clusters of data

A Chicago patrol officer accesses the Illinois Citizen Law Enforcement Analysis and Reporting system (CLEAR) from his patrol car.

On the Job: Becoming a Database Developer

Job Description:

Database developers create programs for data storage, retrieval, and re-porting. They set up and test the function of the database and make adjustments as necessary. They provide support to database administra-tors and cooperate with other database users to ensure the system is sat-isfying their requirements.

Education:

Aspiring database developers are encouraged to obtain a bachelor's de-gree in computer science or another field that has a significant program-ming component, such as mathematics or business administration. Technical and vocational schools also offer two-year diploma programs and one-year certificate programs in the field.

Personal Qualifications:

Aspiring database developers must have a strong interest in computers and be knowledgeable about hardware, software, computer systems, and processes. They should be methodical, logical, patient, careful, and ac-curate. They must also enjoy change, work well under pressure, and work well with others.

Salary:

A beginning database developer can earn between thirty-five and forty-five thousand dollars annually.

in police department computers that might link crimes and give police the information they need to find a perpetrator. Muscarello explains how he studied six of Chicago's most suc-cessful detectives when designing his program:

We picked their brains for the type of patterns they were looking for. We looked at what they did, and found . . . some of them concentrated on the victim, some on the time of day, but they all concentrated on something, and it helped them solve the crime. We picked out the best data features to look at and tried to [program the system to look for patterns the way the human brain does].[60]

National Databases

For those states that cannot or do not want to create their own crime databases, the FBI's National Crime Information Center (NCIC), headquartered in Clarksburg, West Virginia, provides an index of criminal information at no charge to those who wish to use it. Established in 1967 and upgraded in the 1990s, the database includes information regarding fugitives with active arrest warrants, parolees, missing persons, and unidentified human remains as well as firearms records and driver's license information. Designed to complement metropolitan and statewide systems, the NCIC is used by more than ninety-four thousand agencies, including federal, state, local, and tribal law enforcement authorities; members of the U.S. intelligence community; and foreign agencies such as the Royal Canadian Mounted Police. Glenn Woods emphasizes that data-sharing systems are the key to catching today's highly mobile criminal: "If you have murders in Los Angeles, Reno, New York City and El Paso, unless these jurisdictions are entering the cases into a central system, they may never be recognized as being linked to the same offender."[61]

The FBI's Violent Criminal Apprehension Program (ViCAP) is another

By the Numbers

1990s
The decade that the Automated Fingerprint Identification System began to be widely used in the United States.

free nationwide data information center, but it is more specific to murder. Its creator, former Los Angeles detective Pierce Brooks, helped design it to "provide all law enforcement agencies reporting similar-pattern violent crimes with the information necessary to initiate a coordinated multiagency investiga-

The Violent Criminal Apprehension Program

The concept of the Violent Criminal Apprehension Program (ViCAP) originated with Los Angeles police officer Pierce Brooks when he was hunting for serial killer Harvey Glatman in 1956. As Brooks studied two unrelated murder scenes involving young women as victims, he noted similarities in the crimes. He became convinced that one man may have killed both women and could kill again. After hours of newspaper research in local libraries, Brooks found another case that seemed similar to those he was investigating. He went on to make a fingerprint match between the cases and tracked down Glatman.

As a result of his work, Brooks concluded that data about murders should be entered into a computer system where information could be correlated. Open and closed cases could be stored, and investigators could consult the database for similar patterns when they came across a new murder. Brooks suggested that the Los Angeles police department purchase a million-dollar computer to track future serial killers, but his suggestion was ignored. He continued to push his idea and, in 1982, got the attention of the U.S. Department of Justice. Shortly thereafter, ViCAP was created. Former FBI agent Roy Hazelwood remembers, "It was decided that the FBI would run it out of Quantico [Virginia] and in 1985, we hired Brooks to become the first director of ViCAP, because it was his idea."

Quoted in Katherine Ramsland, "Profiling," Crime Library, 2006. www.crimelibrary.com/criminal_mind/profiling/hazelwood/1.html.

tion."[62] When crimes—solved, unsolved, or only attempted—are committed anywhere in the United States, information can be submitted to ViCAP and logged into its system. Investigators who are looking for crimes similar to those in their region can then access the system, focus on a particular method of operating or signature, and perhaps discover that a murder in Los Angeles is linked to one committed in Seattle. Kirk Mellecker, a specialist with ViCAP, says, "If you've got a string of prostitutes dumped across five states and each of them are wearing a red bow tie, that's where we can step in and help police recognize patterns. The main benefit here is that through ViCAP, we're bringing police agencies together."[63]

The most notorious serial killer to be apprehended with the help of ViCAP was the Railroad Killer, Angel Maturino Resendez, who took the lives of eleven people in Kentucky, Illinois, and Texas between 1997 and 1999. Resendez's victims all lived near the railroads he continuously rode throughout the United States, Mexico, and Canada. The illegal immigrant and convicted felon was not immediately suspected in most of the killings, but when information was entered into ViCAP, his name popped up. Authorities apprehended him in July 1999, when he surrendered at the border in El Paso, Texas.

Angel Maturino Resendez, the Railroad Killer, is the most notorious serial killer to be apprehended with the help of the Violent Criminal Apprehension Program (ViCAP).

Incomplete Systems

Even though computers and information technology help law enforcement officials track serial killers, the systems are not perfect and remain a supplement to traditional police methods. Professor Arthur Lurigio, chairman of the Criminal Justice

Department at Loyola University in Chicago, emphasizes, "The technology will never supplant the work of a good police detective. Nothing replaces asking good questions and getting statements from people."[64] Some of the system weaknesses stem from the fact that the databases are incomplete. Not all police departments take the time to input their information. Some report information inaccurately. Some report irregularly.

Some of the databases were improperly created or are difficult to use. For instance, one investigator in Washington State uncovered the fact that the NCIC database never yielded a hit when the search was based on dental records. The problem stemmed from the fact that the NCIC dental form was complicated and subjective, leading authorities who documented missing persons' dental records to make mistakes. Forensic dentist Gary Bell tested the database in 2003 by trying to match the records of four known murder victims whose records had been previously entered into NCIC. The system was unable to come up with a match. Bell, who is an adviser for Washington's Missing and Unidentified Persons Unit, has since helped implement the Computer Aided Postmortem Identification system—a dental comparison program developed by the U.S. Army to help identify war dead—in Washington State. He says, "[The NCIC] just doesn't work. No one I know has ever told me of a single time that it did."[65]

Shortcomings

A shortcoming in IAFIS was revealed in 1999 when authorities discovered that it did not include the U.S. Immigration and Naturalization Service's IDENT fingerprint database. Because of the oversight, when the U.S. Border Patrol apprehended Angel Maturino Resendez for illegal entry into the United States and ran his fingerprints through its system, it did not get the information that the FBI wanted him for murder. The Border Patrol subsequently deported him to Mexico, where a short time later he slipped back across the border and took the lives of four more people. C.G. Almengor, a border supervisor, says, "Our computers told us that he was nothing of lookout material. We really wish he had been in the system so we could have caught him."[66] The two systems have since been integrated, so that Border Patrol searches include both IDENT and IAFIS.

Even when computer programs are complete, they can malfunction. The fingerprints of felon Jeremy Brian Jones were entered into IAFIS while he lived in Oklahoma, but in 2000

A Successful System

Law enforcement personnel know that some criminal computer databases are better than others. One of the best in the United States is San Diego's Automated Regional Justice Information System (ARJIS), described by Raymond Dussault in an article entitled "Shared Books Nab Crooks" on the Government Technology Web site:

ARJIS is a complex computer system which contains information on crime cases, arrests, citations, field interviews, traffic accidents, fraudulent documents, and stolen property. It is used for criminal investigations and statistical information. Investigators can also request notification of information concerning an individual, location, or vehicle

ARJIS is comprised of over 300 computer programs and sub-modules running on a central mainframe [computer]. This system services a network of over 659 computer terminals and printers throughout the 4,265 square miles [11,046 sq. km] of San Diego County. . . . Its ability to gather crime data without respect to jurisdictional lines has led to cost savings and numerous cases solved throughout the greater San Diego region.

Raymond Dussault, "Shared Books Nab Crooks," Government Technology, August 1, 1999. www.govtech.net/magazine/story.php?id=94893&issue=8:1999.

A glitch in the fingerprint database system set Jeremy Brian Jones free to kill again. Here he is pictured with photos of eight possible victims.

he fled to Georgia to avoid arrest for sexual assault and took the name John Paul Chapman. Eventually he was arrested again, and Georgia authorities fingerprinted him and submitted the prints to IAFIS. Instead of matching his prints to existing files and identifying him as a fugitive, the database created a second file under his alias, Chapman. The mistake was not noticed until 2004, after he was apprehended by Alabama authorities for murdering Lisa Nichols, a divorced mother of two. He eventually was charged with three murders and was named a suspect in five others. Georgia Bureau of Investigation assistant deputy director Terry Gibbons defended the system, saying, "It's very infrequent to have this sort of error with automatic fingerprint identification systems now in use."[67]

Other forensic and technology experts agree with Gibbons and are quick to point out that computer systems cannot be made foolproof. Despite instances such as the above, however, they have helped authorities take huge strides in the detection and identification of serial killers. And it is likely that, as files become more complete and as information is increasingly shared, law enforcement will be even more successful, and killers will find it increasingly difficult to get away with murder. Criminologist Jack Levin says, "I think as the technology advances continue, we will see more serial killers being brought to justice."[68] George Vuilleumier, president of the National Association of Chiefs of Police, puts it in layman's terms: "The more we exchange information the worse off the bad guys will be."[69]

Notes

Introduction: With Lethal Intent

1. Quoted in P.J. Huffstutter and Stephanie Simon, "We Have BTK Killer, Kansas Police Say Dennis Rader, a Father and Scout Leader, Is Suspected of Torturing and Killing 10 People," *Orlando* (FL) *Sentinel*, February 27, 2005, p. A1.

2. Shirley Lynn Scott, "Monsters or Victims?" Crime Library, 2006. www.crimelibrary.com/serial_killers/notorious/tick/victims_1.html.

3. Quoted in Jason Kravarik, "Who Is Dennis Rader?" KSN.com, February 26, 2005. www.ksn.com/news/stories/7036051.html.

4. David Reichert, *Chasing the Devil*. New York: Little, Brown, 2004, p. 125.

Chapter 1: Monster Hunters

5. Jan Bouchard-Kerr, "Suspected," Crime Library, 2006. www.crimelibrary.com/serial_killers/predators/olson/9.html.

6. John Philpin, "To Catch a Killer: A Field Guide to the Baton Rouge Serial Murder Investigation," KariSable.com, 2003. www.karisable.com/skazbr2.htm.

7. Ann Rule, *Green River, Running Red*. New York: Free, 2004, p. 328.

8. Quoted in Ted Schwarz, *The Hillside Strangler*. Sanger, CA: Quill Driver, 2004, p. 69.

9. Quoted in Mike Barber, "Serial Killers Prey on the 'Less Dead,'" Seattle PI.com, February 20, 2003. http://seattlepi.nwsource.com/local/108705_predators20.shtml.

10. Ann Rule, *Lust Killer*. New York: Penguin, 1983, pp. 105–106.

11. Quoted in Burl Barer, *Body Count*. New York: Pinnacle, 2002, p. 142.

12. Sherri Rogalski, "Green River Debacle: It Could Have Happened to Anyone," *Seattle Times*, February 26, 1986, p. A11.

13. Quoted in Tim Potter, "Flexible Interviewers Glean Most from Suspects," *Wichita Eagle*, March 4, 2005. www.kansas.com/mld/kansas/news/special_packages/btk/archive/11048066.htm.

14. Schwarz, *The Hillside Strangler*, p. 53.

15. Quoted in Robert Beattie, *Nightmare in Wichita: The Hunt for the BTK Strangler*. New York: New American Library, 2005, p. 104.

16. Quoted in Rule, *Green River, Running Red*, pp. 222–23.

17. Quoted in Jeannette White and Bill Morlin, "Cops Yanked from Case—Police Chief Surprises Community When He Pulls Back from Task Force, Citing Budget Shortfall," *Spokane* (WA) *Spokesman-Review*, July 22, 2001, p. B1.

18. Quoted in Katherine Ramsland, "Always Learning," Crime Library, 2006. www.crimelibrary.com/criminal_mind/profiling/history_method/new_22.html.

Chapter 2: Probing the Minds of Killers

19. Quoted in Wayne Petherick, "Historical Overview," Crime Library, 2006. www.crimelibrary.com/criminal_mind/profiling/profiling2/2.html.

20. Quoted in Thomas R. O'Connor, "History of Profiling," North Carolina Wesleyan College, 2006. http://faculty.ncwc.edu/TOConnor/428/428lect01.htm.

21. Robert K. Ressler and Tom Shachtman, *Whoever Fights Monsters: My Twenty Years Tracking Serial Killers for the FBI.* New York: St. Martin's, 1992, p. 156.

22. Robert D. Keppel and William J. Birnes, *Signature Killers: Interpreting the Calling Cards of the Serial Murderer.* New York: Pocket, 1997, p. 5.

23. Quoted in Natasha Mitchell, "In the Mind of the Psychopath," ABC.net, 2006. www.abc.net.au/rn/science/mind/s511461.htm.

24. Rule, *Lust Killer,* p. 122.

25. Katherine Ramsland, "Hunting the Vampire," Crime Library, 2006. www.crimelibrary.com/serial_killers/weird/chase/vampire_5.html.

26. Keppel and Birnes, *Signature Killers,* pp. 26–27.

27. Quoted in Katherine Ramsland, "Geographic Profiling 101: Approaching a Case," Crime Library, 2006. www.crimelibrary.com/criminal_mind/profiling/geographic/3.html.

28. Quoted in Barer, *Body Count,* p. 311.

29. Quoted in Bill McGarigle, "Crime Profilers Gain New Weapons," *Government Technology,* December 1997. www.vgin.virginia.gov/documents/articles/localgovt/Crime%20Profilers_Gain_New_Weapons.htm.

30. Quoted in Katherine Ramsland, "The Mind Hunters," Crime Library, 2006. www.crimelibrary.com/criminal_mind/profiling/history_method/6.html.

Chapter 3: Getting the Word Out

31. Marilyn Bardsley, "Ressler's Interview," Crime Library, 2006. www.crimelibrary.com/serial_killers/notorious/berkowitz/23.htm.

32. Quoted in Bill Morlin, "Task Force Pleads for Secrecy—More than One Reporter Decides Not to Run Stories When Detectives Say They Will Jeopardize the Case," *Spokane* (WA) *Spokesman-Review*, July 26, 2001, p. B3.

33. Quoted in Bill Morlin and Jeannette

White, "Admitting the Truth—with the Discovery of Shawn Johnson's Body, Detectives Can No Longer Hope the Murders Are Unrelated," *Spokane* (WA) *Spokesman-Review*, July 5, 2001, p. B1.

34. Carlton Smith and Tomas Guillen, *The Search for the Green River Killer*. New York: Signet, 2004, p. 80.

35. Quoted in Smith and Guillen, *The Search for the Green River Killer*, p. 349.

36. Quoted in Katherine Ramsland, "Too Easy to Criticize a Difficult Manhunt," DeSales University, 2006. www.allencol. edu/default.aspx?pageid=232.

37. Quoted in Barer, *Body Count*, pp. 261–62.

38. Quoted in Mark Fuhrman, *Murder in Spokane: Catching a Serial Killer*. New York: Cliff Street, 2001, p. 229.

39. David Kaczynski, "The Death Penalty Up Close and Personal," New Yorkers Against the Death Penalty, 2006. www. nyadp.org/main/david.html.

40. Quoted in Beattie, *Nightmare in Wichita*, p. 321.

41. Quoted in Mike Roarke, "Psychics Offer Their Services. Cops Listen, but Stop Short of Searching Cheney Tunnels," *Spokane* (WA) *Spokesman-Review*, July 15, 2001, p. B3.

42. Quoted in Jason Kravarik, "Police Swab Retired Officers," KSN.com, November 22, 2004. http://ksn.com/news/stories/6556806.html.

43. Stanley Crouch, "US Is Still Land of Law and Order," Booker Rising, October 30, 2005. http://bookerrising. blogspot.com/2005_10_01_bookerris ing_archive.html.

Chapter 4: Relying on Science

44. Quoted in Smith and Guillen, *The Search for the Green River Killer*, p. 300.

45. Quoted in Perkin Elmer, "Moving IR Spectroscopy Down to the Micron Level Puts Serial Killer Behind Bars," 2005. http://las.perkinelmer.com/Content/Rel atedMaterials/IRSpectroscopySerialKille rCST.pdf.

46. Quoted in Mike Roarke, "Botanist Identifies Trees in Killer's Yard— Finding the Yard Was Another Story," *Spokane* (WA) *Spokesman-Review*, July 9, 2001, p. A8.

47. Quoted in Bill Morlin and Jeannette White, "Crawling with Cops— Detectives Begin Search of Robert Yates' Home, but the Best Evidence Would Come from a Lab," *Spokane* (WA) *Spokesman-Review*, July 27, 2001, p. B1.

48. Katherine Ramsland, Quoted in "The Techniques," Crime Library, 2006. www.crimelibrary.com/criminal_mind/ forensics/finger prints/4.html.

49. Quoted in Steven Kroft, "Forensic Evidence; Skepticism Surrounding Dr. Michael West's Use of Bite Mark Analysis in Murder Cases," *60 Minutes*, February 17, 2003. www.law-forensic. com/cfr_west_14.htm.

50. Shannon Rasp, "Taking a Bite Out of Crime," *Health Leader*, October 31, 2005. www.uthouston.edu/hleader/

archive/Oral_Health/2005/forensicden
tistry-1031.html.

51. Quoted in Rasp, "Taking a Bite Out of Crime."

52. Katherine Ramsland, "The Most Famous Bite," Crime Library, 2006. www.crime library.com/forensics/bitemarks.

53. Quoted in Katherine Ramsland, "Identification," Crime Library, 2006. www.crimelibrary.com/criminal_mind/f orensics/anthropology/2.html?sect=21.

54. Quoted in Richard Roth, "How Do Serial Killer Suspects Elude Police?" CNN.com, June 24, 1999. www.cnn. com/US/9906 /24/serial.mo.

55. Quoted in Raymond Dussault, "Shared Books Nab Crooks," Government Technology, August 1, 1999. www.govtech. net/magazine/story.php?id=94893&sto ry_pg=2.

Chapter 5: High-Tech Tactics

56. Quoted in Patrick Bellamy, "On the Trail of Ted Bundy," Crime Library, 2006. www.crimelibrary.com/criminal _mind/profiling /keppel1/1.html.

57. Quoted in Heidi Kriz, "Sharpening Up Technology," Wired News, January 27, 1999. www.wired.com/news/technolo gy/0,1282,17565,00.html.

58. Quoted in Kevin Davis, "Knowledge on the Beat," Destination KM.com, July 1999. www.destinationkm.com/articles/ default. asp?ArticleID=87.

59. Quoted in Vince Beiser, "Thinking Like a Serial Killer," Wired News, July 1,

1999. www.wired.com/news/technolo gy/0,1282, 19940,00.html.

60. Quoted in Jim McKay, "Brain Power," Government Technology, May 2, 2006. www.govtech.net/magazine/story.php?id =99373 &story_pg=2.

61. Quoted in McGarigle, "Crime Profilers Gain New Weapons."

62. Quoted in Criminal Profiling, "The New ViCAP," February 2005. www. criminalprofiling.com/The-New- ViCAP_s319.html.

63. Quoted in Barber, "Serial Killers Prey on the 'Less Dead.'"

64. Quoted in Davis, "Knowledge on the Beat."

65. Quoted in Lewis Kamb, "After 21 Years, the Bones Get a Name," Seattle Post-Intelligencer, February 26, 2003, p. A1.

66. Quoted in Joseph Geringer, "Manhunt," Crime Library, 2006. www.crimelibrary. com/serial_killers/notorious/resendez /manhunt_2.html.

67. Quoted in PhillyBurbs.com, "FBI Mistakes Allow GA Suspect to Go Free," May 4, 2005. www.phillyburbs. com/pb-dyn/news/278-05042005- 484859.html.

68. Quoted in Allen G. Breed, "Science, Hard Work Corner Serial Killers," Vancouver (WA) Columbian, April 26, 2004, p. A7.

69. Quoted in Alan D. Fischer, "COPLINK Nabs Criminals Faster," Arizona Daily Star, January 7, 2001. http://ai.bpa.ari zona.edu/go/recognition/azstar0101. htm.

For More Information

Books

Burl Barer, *Body Count: The Terrifying True Story of the Spokane Serial Killer.* New York: Pinnacle, 2002. Relates how investigators successfully tracked and captured Spokane serial killer Robert Lee Yates Jr.

Robert Beattie, *Nightmare in Wichita: The Hunt for the BTK Strangler.* New York: New American Library, 2005. Attorney Beattie shares his inside knowledge of the BTK case and how police finally identified and arrested the killer.

N.E. Genge, *The Forensic Casebook.* New York: Ballantine, 2002. A relatively lively look at forensics. Includes chapters on evidence, the corpse, and specialties such as odontology and photography.

Donald M. Holmes and Stephen T. Holmes, *Murder in America.* Thousand Oaks, CA: Sage, 1994. Examines various types of homicide, including serial murder. Presents trends, motives, methods, statistics, and other information.

Michael Newton, *The Encyclopedia of Serial Killers.* New York: Facts On File, 2000. Gives brief descriptions of hundreds of serial killers, ranging from African American serial killer Howard Allen to German-born Anna Maria Zwanziger.

David Reichert, *Chasing the Devil.* New York: Little, Brown, 2004. The story of the Green River Killer investigation, told by one of the men who tracked and apprehended him.

Web Sites

Combined DNA Index System (CODIS) Web Site (www.fbi.gov/hq/lab/codis/clickmap.htm). Provides brochures, statistics, investigations aided by CODIS, and links to FBI pages.

Crime Library, Court TV (www.crimelibrary.com/index.html). A collection of more than six hundred nonfiction feature stories by prominent writers on major crimes, criminals, trials, forensics, and criminal profiling.

FBI Crime Laboratory (www.fbi.gov/hq/lab/labhome.htm). Includes a history of the crime laboratory as well as procedures for submitting evidence, guidelines for a crime scene search, and descriptions of various types of evidence.

Kari Sable's True Crime and Justice Web Site (www.karisable.com/crime.htm). Includes reviews of true-crime books and information and discussion on serial killers and other topics.

Index

Italic page locators indicate images; page locators followed by *m* indicate maps.

Picture Credits

About the Author

Diane Yancey lives in the Pacific Northwest with her husband, Michael; their dog, Gelato; and their cats, Lily and Newton. She has written more than twenty-five books for middle-grade and high-school readers, including *Murder*, *The Forensic Anthropologist*, and *The Case of the Green River Killer*.